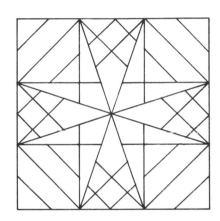

THE FRIENDSHIP QUILT BOOK

THE FRIENDSHIP QUILT BOOK

Step-by-step instructions for making your own quilt —
from the distinctive designs of 20 nationally known quilters.

by Mary Golden

A division of Yankee Publishing Incorporated
Dublin, New Hampshire

Book design by Jill Shaffer
Illustrated by Ray Maher

Photographs by Joel Kaplan, p. 16; David Donoho, p. 36; Charles Collins, p. 50; Mager R. Greenough, p. 58; Doug Mindell, pp. 66-70, 72; Stephen O. Muskie, p. 71.

The quotes on p. 122 and p. 146 from *By Shaker Hands* by June Sprigg, copyright 1975, are reprinted by permission of Alfred A. Knopf, Inc.

Yankee Publishing Incorporated
Dublin, New Hampshire
First Edition
Second Printing, 1985
Copyright 1985 by Yankee Publishing Incorporated

Library of Congress Catalogue Card Number: 84-51788
ISBN: 0-89909-062-1

Dedicated to
Chassie and our family of friends

Nature produced us related to one another, since she created us from the same source and to the same end. She engendered in us mutual affection and made us prone to friendships. . . . Through her orders, our hands are ready to help in the good work. Our relations with one another are like a stone arch, which would collapse if the stones did not mutually support each other, and which is upheld in this very way.

Seneca

Acknowledgments

Besides the quiltmakers who so generously contributed their designs, essays, photos, biographical information, and, of course, their valuable time, there was an equally giving group of Crossroads Quilters who shared their quiltmaking talents, time, support, and culinary skills. Within that group and deserving special attention is Maureen Walker, whose careful needlework is evident in all of the embroidery on the quilt. As time grew short, a close group of Maureen's friends rallied round her and helped complete the embroidering. Thank you to Irene Bean, Kathy Doane, Jackie Downs, Calista Greenough, Opal Jacobson, Lorna Kapantais, Shan Lear, Roxie Poitras, Gertrude Storch, Hugh Walker, Gloria Webster, and Nancy Whitney.

I would also like to express my appreciation to Nancy Halpern and Joyce Gross, who were especially helpful in locating quiltmakers from outside the New England region; Shan Lear, Nancy Anketell, and Susie Astolfi, who coordinated my plans with the Crossroads Quilters; Roxie Poitras, who graciously lent her quilt scrapbooks for gems of wisdom; Gwen Wells, who supplied the Crossroads biography; and my weekly Stitch and Bitch pals, who lent their encouragement, as did my good friend Vivian Ritter.

The staff of Yankee Publishing Incorporated are to be highly praised for their patience and encouragement — especially Sandy Taylor, who is now more than my editor; she is my friend and budding quiltmaker. She made my first writing experience a joy.

And finally an acknowledgment to my husband, Harrison, and the rest of my family of friends for every positive thought.

Editor's Note: As with the friendship quilt, which has touched so many people across the country — from the quiltmakers who sent their favorite designs to those who made the blocks and others who embroidered the individuals' names — so has this book project involved people from coast to coast. We would like to thank Virginia Avery, who corresponded with us about the book idea when it was in its earliest stages, and Jean Ray Laury, who gave us precious time between quilting classes to offer further suggestions. True to the spirit of quiltmaking, they both shared their thoughts and enthusiasm.

Contents

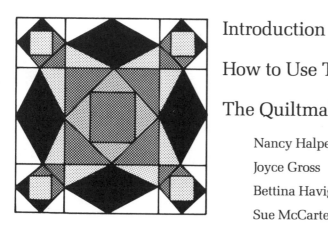

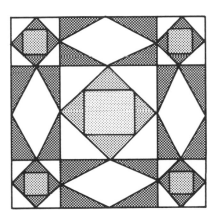

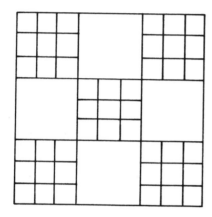

Friendship is the golden
thread that ties the hearts of
all the world.

John Evelyn

Introduction

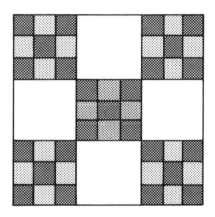

What is a friendship quilt? In its broadest sense, it is a quilt given by one or several friends to another as a token of that friendship. In its simplest form, the quilt can be any size at all and sewn by only one friend, using one pattern. By traditional definition, however, a true friendship quilt consists of different designs and fabrics, sewn by different friends, and assembled by a group.

The friendship quilt is a material testament of women's strong friendship ties throughout American history. At her best, the American woman, in the group process, has displayed the talents of design, forethought, purpose, industriousness, altruism, frugality, and generosity. When scrapbags have been searched, fabric and time donated, what would have taken one woman countless hours of solitary work has taken a group of women less time, at a fraction of the cost and with good memories in the doing and giving of the quilt.

The friendship quilt survives because the need for quilts and need for friendship survives. Warmth and love nourish our bodies and souls. These are essential ingredients of everyday life as well as special requirements in hard times. America's beginnings were especially difficult, its transformations difficult, and so it is no surprise that we find the American quilt tradition as a continuous social element.

Through quiltmaking a genuine respect develops among people. Friendships built on this mutual respect instill a sense of security and self-confidence. Quiltmakers encourage quilt lovers to try their hands at it. Mothers teach daughters, daughters sometimes teach mothers, friends teach friends.

A special language exists among quiltmakers. Their words and thoughts are expressed in the patterns, fabrics, quilting designs, and colors that they use in their quilts. To know their quilts is to understand them in a very special way.

In the process of working on this book, a friendship quilt was conceived, planned, sewn, and completed. Twenty very generous women from across the country, whose lives have been greatly affected and enriched by quiltmaking, shared their favorite designs and thoughts on friendship. An equally special group of New England quiltmakers from the Crossroads Quilters Guild of Wenham, Massachusetts, shared their enthusiasm, thoughts, and time by fashioning quilt blocks from these designs, sewing them together, and creating this friendship quilt. The entire process of making the quilt has been recorded here as a guide to channeling desire and enthusiasm to a successful and beautiful conclusion. At the same time, there was an opportunity to gain new talents, new friends, and new memories.

"Our" quilt, a symbol of unity among quilters, will be preserved in The New England Quilters Guild Museum as a testament to the art of quiltmaking and to the value placed on the friendship that exists among us today.

Mary Golden

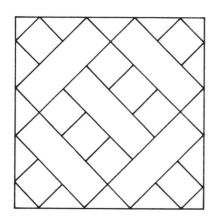

*The language of friendship is
not words but meanings.*
Henry David Thoreau

How to Use This Book

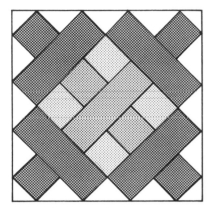

After reading about the quiltmakers and their designs, refer to the chapter on Choosing a Design/Choosing a Project (page 73), followed by Color Choice/Fabric Choice (page 77).

Once you've chosen your project and the colors and fabrics you plan to use, spend some time on "behind the scenes" work in preparation for sewing. This includes making templates, arranging the designs within the project, purchasing supplies, and preparing and cutting the fabrics. Carefully read the Templates chapter (page 81), then review the information on the block(s) you've chosen. After preparing the templates and cutting the pieces, Assembling the Quilt (page 107) will be your next step. Read through the whole chapter first, check the quilt top arrangement for last-minute changes, then begin piecing the top. Before doing the sandwiching, be sure to read the Quilting and Binding chapters (pages 123 and 127). They will not only give you quilting templates and binding suggestions and the best time to apply each, but will offer ways to approach the quilting which may be worth pondering while you are piecing the quilt top.

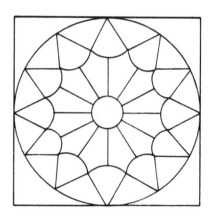

Friendship's a word to few confined
The offspring of a noble mind
A generous warmth which fills the breast
And better felt than e'er expressed.
Author unknown

The Quiltmakers and Their Patterns

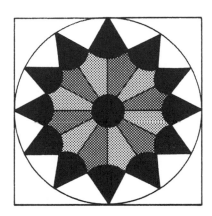

The United States has thousands of quiltmakers, and each region has a distinctive style just as each quiltmaker has a distinctive style. Twenty quiltmakers from across the country introduce themselves to you here, not only through their favorite patterns, but also through their thoughts on friendship. In addition, you will meet some of the members of the Crossroads Quilters Guild from Wenham, Massachusetts. Each of these women selected 1 of the 20 patterns, fashioned it into a block, then worked on assembling all the blocks into the finished friendship quilt.

There are twenty 12″ designs on the following pages — some original and some traditional. (There is also a 21st design, and a discussion of this appears later, on page 58.) The designs represent a wide range of techniques from strip piecing to appliqué. Some have more pieces than others, though, in all cases, the basic techniques are simple. With very little practice, all of the patterns in this book can be mastered, although some will take a little longer to complete than others. Detailed instructions on the techniques involved are included in later chapters.

Each design has a name and each makes use of certain shapes called templates. The templates are shown full-sized (unless otherwise noted) and most do not include seam allowances. Do not be discouraged or intimidated by a pattern with a number of templates and pieces. *Storm at Sea* (page 42), with 8 templates and 65 pieces, has no center and thus no convergence of seams at a center point as does *Seashell* (page 28), with 6 templates and 11 pieces; therefore, *Storm at Sea* is technically "easier." The curved seams of the *Breadfruit* design (page 18), with 1 template and 1 piece, will take longer to appliqué than the *Cherokee Rose* (page 37), with 4 templates and 8 pieces, plus the stem. The number of templates or pieces does not determine the design's degree of difficulty.

When 1 or more of the 12″ blocks is used for a project, it is arranged in a 'set.' Suggested 'sets' for small- to large-sized projects using 1 to 20 blocks are found in later chapters. When all 20 blocks are sewn together in the patchwork 'set' suggested here, they will yield a quilt measuring 96″x96″. (Turn to page 72 to see the completed friendship quilt.)

Nancy Halpern

NATICK, MASSACHUSETTS

Nancy Halpern began making quilts in the early 1970s and is now involved throughout the country with quiltmaking in all its diverse forms — sewing, teaching, lecturing, writing, photographing, sharing, and promoting. Her quilts have been shown in national quilting and fiber arts publications, on television, and in numerous exhibits.

"I am sure that the warmth and strength of quilts comes less from the fabrics and batting that make them than from the gifts they incorporate, embody, and convey. Some of my quilts begin with a gift of fabric, and most have been finished with presents that arrive by mail or in the hands of friends. Then these quilts, either privately or publicly, become new gifts, transferring the spirit of the gifts with which they were made. Many years ago, two students gave me a fragile old quilt top they had been ordered to cut up for clothing. Today it radiates the love with which it was made, saved, given, and received. It is faded and thin, but I am brighter and warmer."

Archipelago
ORIGINAL PATCHWORK DESIGN

Fabric Requirements:
Variety of light, medium, and dark prints, stripes, and solids

Shan Lear of Manchester, Massachusetts, chose Nancy Halpern's original contemporary design for several reasons. She knew her personally, was closely acquainted with Nancy's quilt of the same name ("Archipelago"), and had heard Nancy speak on landscape and architecture at a 1983 meeting of the Crossroads Quilters Guild in Wenham, Massachusetts.

Since the *Archipelago* block is not symmetrical in color or shape and only suggests rocks, trees, and sky, fabric choice is a personal matter. After choosing and cutting fabrics, pin them onto a sheet of paper as a constant reminder of their correct placement.

Templates E, F, and G are asymmetrical shapes and therefore *must* be placed with the correct side of the template on the wrong side of the fabric. The sewing progression is as follows:

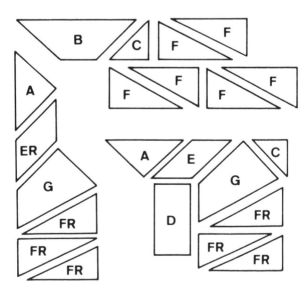

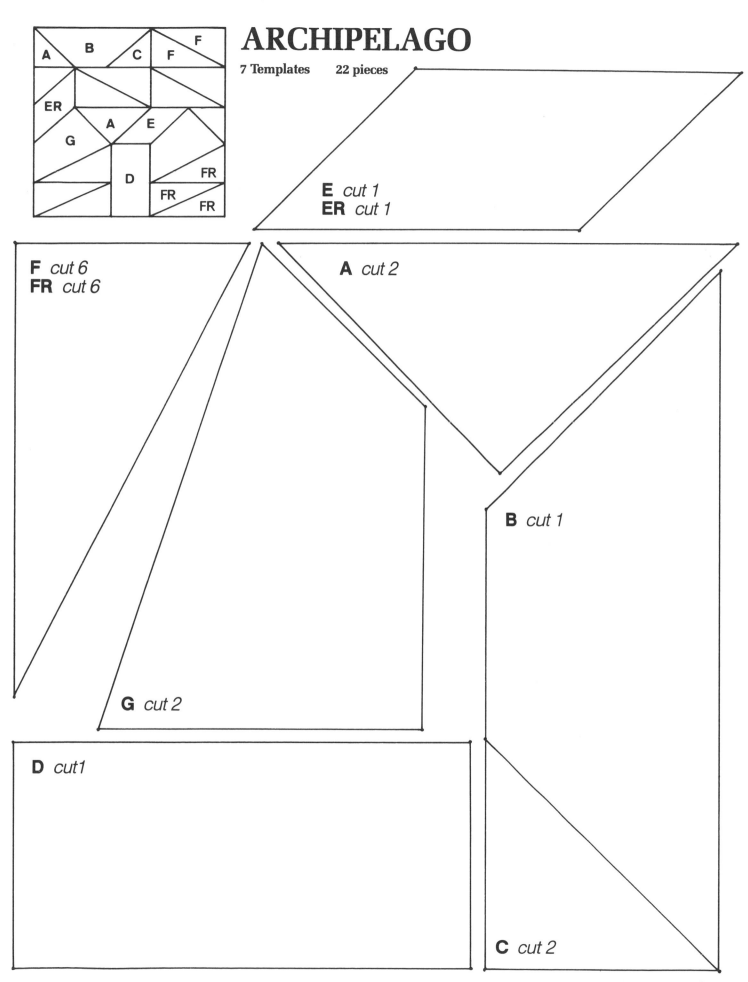

ARCHIPELAGO

7 Templates   **22 pieces**

E *cut 1*
ER *cut 1*

F *cut 6*
FR *cut 6*

A *cut 2*

B *cut 1*

G *cut 2*

D *cut1*

C *cut 2*

Joyce Gross

MILL VALLEY, CALIFORNIA

Joyce Gross is editor/publisher of the *Quilters' Journal*, a quarterly publication devoted to the history of quilts, quiltmakers, and textiles. She is primarily interested in the 20th-century world of quilts and has a large collection of quilts, quilt blocks, and literature of that period. Her ultimate goal is to establish a quilt study center for those interested in the history of quilts and persons important to the quilt field.

Joyce's interest in Hawaiian quilts dates back to 1973, when she went to the Honolulu Academy of Arts Quilt Exhibit and fell in love with the art form. She has given lectures and workshops on the subject throughout the United States.

Since 1973 Joyce has been actively promoting an appreciation for quilts and quilting by sponsoring classes, workshops, lectures, tours, and quilt exhibits, as well as publishing the *Quilters' Journal*.

"I have found that quilt lovers are special people. Whether they are quiltmakers, historians, pattern collectors, quilt collectors, or just lovers of quilts, they are for the most part warm, sharing, happy, and friendly people. Many quilt lovers will tell you that they had explored many interests in their lifetimes, but when they found quilts and quiltmaking, they felt as if all of their interests and talents had come together 'at home.'

"It was certainly true for me, and I am happy to be 'at home' with my friends and quilts."

Breadfruit

TRADITIONAL APPLIQUÉ DESIGN/HAWAIIAN APPLIQUÉ

Fabric Requirements:
13″ square base block of light fabric
12″ square of medium, medium-dark, or dark of a solid or fine print

Like Joyce Gross, Mary Ciulla of Gloucester, Massachusetts, also has a deep respect and love for the Hawaiian quilt tradition; thus, she chose this pattern.

The *Breadfruit* design is pictured as being folded into ⅛ of its full size. This ⅛ template can be placed on the ⅛ fold of the 12″ square fabric as is, or, from this small size, a full pattern can be made and drawn onto the unfolded 12″ square. Seam allowances *are* included in this pattern. Follow the basic rules of appliqué found in the chapter Appliqué Designs (page 99).

BREADFRUIT

1 Template   1 Piece   Seam allowances included

Crease line

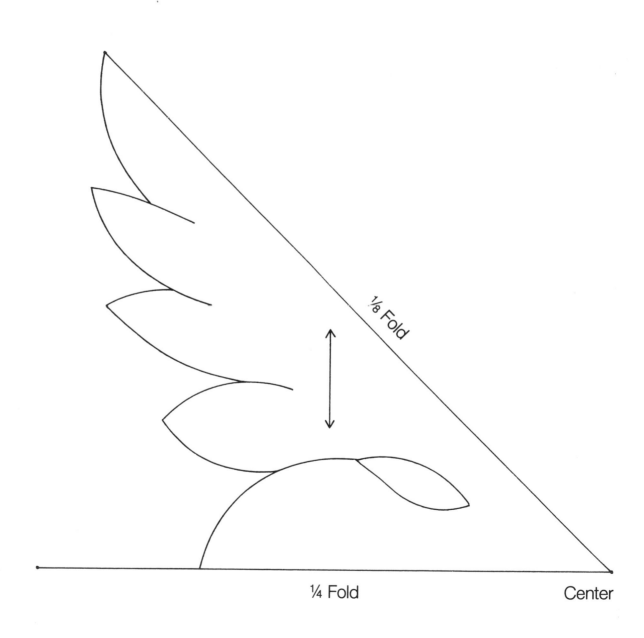

⅛ Fold

¼ Fold

Center

Bettina Havig
COLUMBIA, MISSOURI

Bettina Havig began quilting in 1970, teaching quilting in 1974, and running her own business — The Quilt Cottage — in 1977. She travels frequently, lecturing and conducting workshops on Amish quilts and quilting techniques, garment embellishment, and scrap-quilt planning. As director of the Missouri Quilt Project, she searches for Missouri's heritage in quilts.

"Quilting is sharing. You share your ideas with your friends who quilt; you share your design, color, and technique. A quilter shares her time and talent with the family and friends who receive the quilts, who in turn share the quilts with friends who can appreciate the work and fine stitching.

"Quilting has been a vehicle I've used to meet people throughout the country and to share ideas and skills. It has afforded me an opportunity to travel and share what I have learned with new quilting friends.

"I could not quilt if I could not share."

Cottage Star
ORIGINAL PATCHWORK DESIGN

Fabric Requirements:
Light for the background
Medium, medium-dark, and
    dark prints of varying scale

The name of Bettina Havig's design was inspired by her shop, The Quilt Cottage, in Columbia, Missouri. When Marie Anderson of South Hamilton, Massachusetts, pieced Bettina's block, she noted that the small D/DR triangle is asymmetrical, having 3 sides of varying length. So, when pieces B and C are cut into templates, mark on both where D lies (see dots). The longer side of D (cx) is always pieced to a C and the shorter side (bx) is always pieced to a B. The sewing progression is as follows:

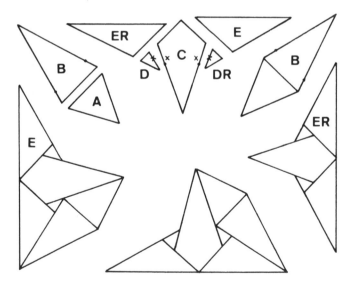

COTTAGE STAR

5 Templates   28 Pieces

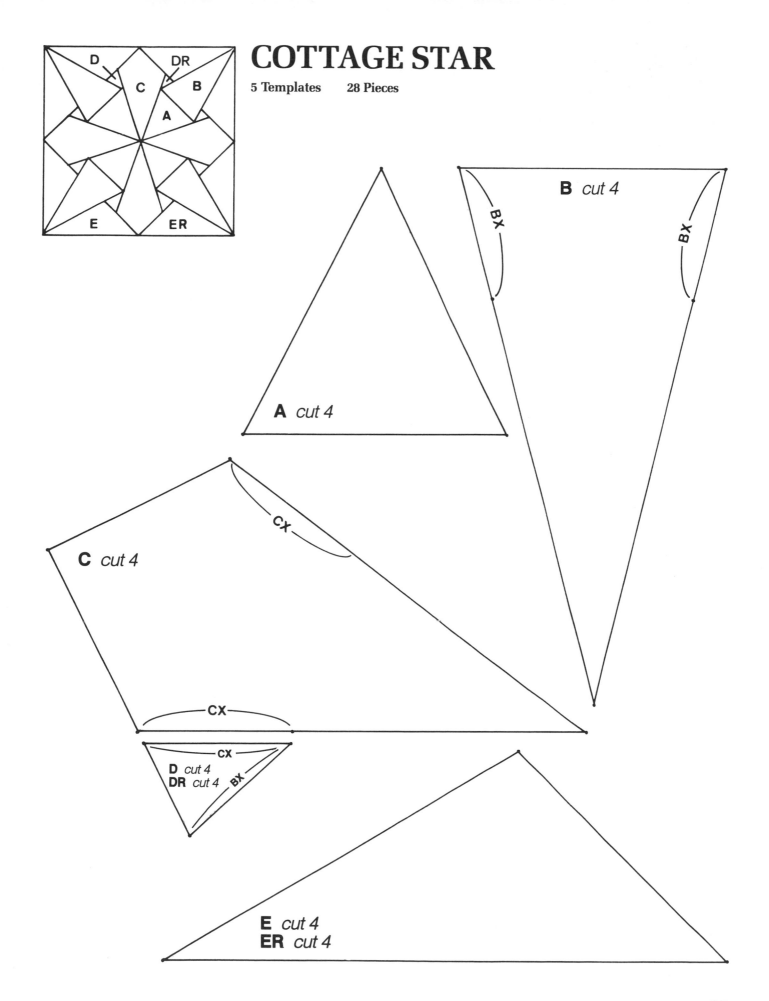

B *cut 4*

BX   BX

A *cut 4*

CX

C *cut 4*

CX

CX

D *cut 4*
DR *cut 4*   BX

E *cut 4*
ER *cut 4*

Sue McCarter
CHARLOTTE, NORTH CAROLINA

Sue McCarter has been quilting since 1973 and has taught both in North Carolina and in the Midwest. She was a guest lecturer at the 1979 Continental Quilting Congress in Washington, D.C., and has taught workshops at 2 of the North Carolina Quilt Symposiums. In 1976 she chaired the group that created the North Carolina Bicentennial Quilt for the Charlotte Symphony Designer House. Her work has been exhibited nationally, and published in *Lady's Circle Patchwork Quilts* and *Quilters' Journal*. Sue is co-author and co-designer (with Judy Bryan) of the pattern "The Bridal Quilt: A Woman's Legacy." She has appeared on several local television programs and on the PBS series "Lap Quilting" with Georgia Bonesteel. Founder and past president of the Charlotte Quilters' Guild, she serves on the Board of Directors of the North Carolina Quilt Symposium, Inc.

Sue is married to John McCarter and has 3 children: Laura, Amy, and Daniel.

"I used to wonder whether it was fate or one of my past misdeeds that demanded retribution. Whichever the case, for most of my life I have been troubled by my close association with talented people, especially the artistic types. All my early role models were gifted: one grandmother painted, another was a concert pianist, and my mother excelled at everything. I broke a lot of crayons and persuaded music teachers to try another profession. Most of the self-esteem that I managed to scrape together was based on virtues — dull stuff like patience, maturity, and good manners. But I always harbored the dream that somewhere deep inside my normal exterior lurked an artist capable of something beautiful.

"As a young, married woman, I turned my attention to a series of energy-intensive projects. They covered the whole range, from macrame to tole painting, and swiftly found themselves featured in garage sales and as Christmas gifts. (It's the thought that counts.) In 1973, my mother introduced me to quilting, and it has proved to be her grandest gift since giving me birth. She had recently discovered the art herself, and our skills and knowledge developed together. Over the years, not only have our skills with patchwork, appliqué, and quilting blossomed, but so has a unique relationship between mother and daughter, built on a mutual love of quilting. We spend hours talking on the phone (long distance, no less) about our current and future quilting projects, and the highlight of each year is our "vacation" together at a quilting convention in some part of the country.

"Quiltmaking throughout history has enabled women not only to provide warmth for their families, but also to give full expression to the beauty in their hearts and minds. It is often a solitary activity, but it has endured because of women's willingness to share their knowledge with others. In an era of water beds, electric heat, and disposable everything, spending 200 hours to make a quilt may indeed seem to be an anachronism. But as for the people who know who they are and who stubbornly celebrate enduring values — they keep on quilting."

Fabric Requirements:
- 13″ square base block of light fabric
- 12″ square for the cut-out appliqué shape of medium, medium-dark, or dark print or solid
- Scraps of a medium-dark solid or fine print for reverse areas

Double Hearts
ORIGINAL APPLIQUÉ/REVERSE APPLIQUÉ DESIGN

Sue McCarter's *Double Hearts*, designed with Judy Bryan, is a cut-paper design with reverse appliqué which adds dimension, interest, and a third color. Jackie Downs of Swampscott, Massachusetts, chose this pattern, which is, as shown, ¼ of the design and can be cut from a folded 12″ square of fabric. Seam allowances *are* included in this pattern. If you prefer, a full template can be made and the full design cut from an unfolded 12″ square of fabric. For details on traditional and reverse appliqué, turn to the chapter on Appliqué Designs, page 99.

DOUBLE HEARTS

1 Template   13 Pieces   Seam allowances included

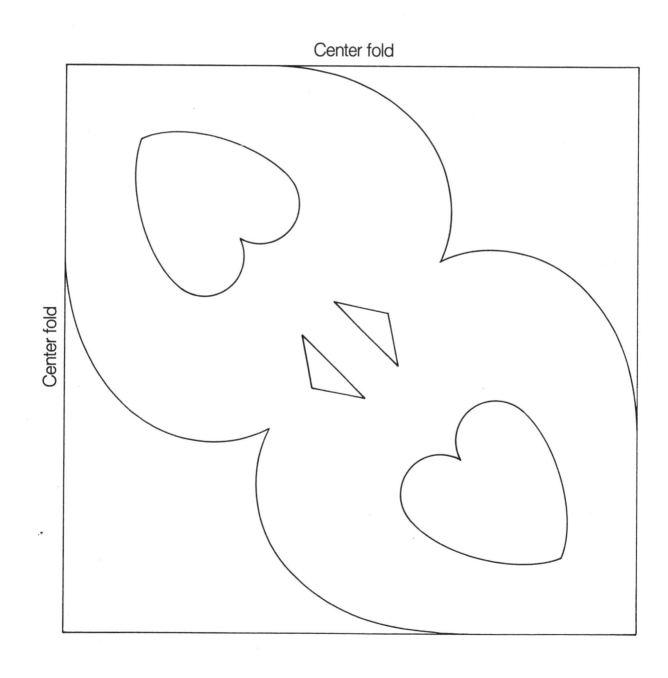

Center fold

Center fold

Mona Barker
KANSAS CITY, MISSOURI

A North Carolina native, Mona Barker has lived in Kansas City, Missouri, for the past 30 years. She has 4 children (including Sue Barker McCarter, see page 22), and 9 grandchildren. Since 1975 her all-consuming interest has been the many facets of quilting, concentrating on symbolism and religious influences evident in antique and contemporary quilts.

"When I discovered quilting, I found a storehouse of delights. The challenge of perfecting each technique and the opportunity to combine them in an unending kaleidoscope of variations fulfilled my longing for creative expression. Sharing these joys with my daughter has brought us closer, a very special treasure indeed. The friendship of the myriad of quilters I have come to know and love is a continuing source of inspiration, and to be a living link between quilters of antiquity and those of the future is a great privilege. I've found a treasure trove; quiltmaking has become my secret drawer."

Secret Drawer
TRADITIONAL PATCHWORK DESIGN

Fabric Requirements:
Light background
Medium, medium-dark, and dark prints of varying scale, with the possibility of a large isolated print for the center

Secret Drawer is a traditional patchwork design that Mona Barker chose for the significance of its name; Grace Marino of Gloucester, Massachusetts, chose it for its straightforward piecing. The design varies according to color and fabric placement. Grace chose to emphasize the center and corner areas with the dark fabric, leaving the medium fabric for the bow-tie side shapes. Ecology cloth (or muslin) was used to form a background consistent with all of the other blocks. The sewing progression is as follows:

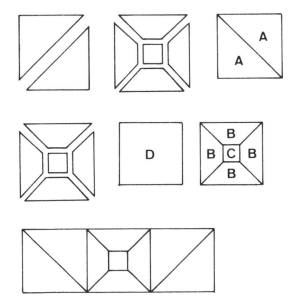

SECRET DRAWER

4 Templates **29 Pieces**

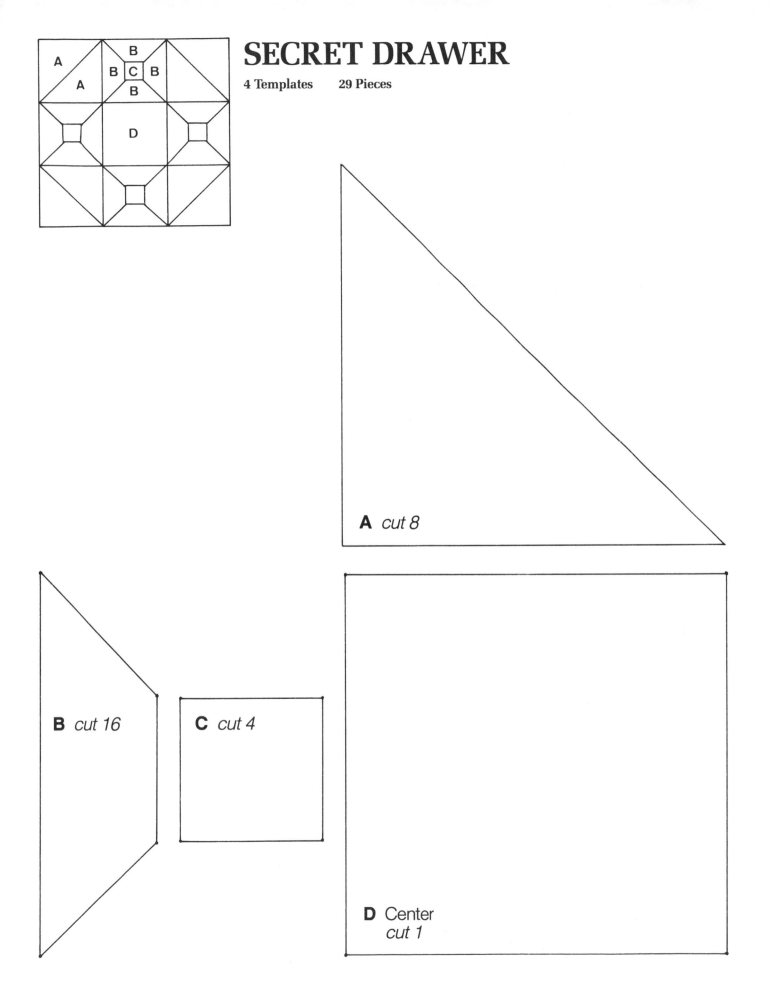

A cut 8

B cut 16

C cut 4

D Center
cut 1

Helen Kelley
MINNEAPOLIS, MINNESOTA

Helen Kelley is an author, designer, lecturer, and teacher. A self-taught quilter, she began exploring the creative possibilities of quilts 35 years ago. She has a particular interest in friendship quilts because of the joyous sharing they foster. Currently, Helen is assembling her 14th friendship quilt.

"I have never seen a friendship basket. Or a friendship rug. No friendship weavings or friendship embroideries. But I have seen friendship quilts, hundreds of them. They are quilts that salute special people, bless marriages, celebrate babies, and honor special occasions. They exalt all aspects of the human condition — joy, affection, sorrow, tenderness. All of these quilts carry a single message: 'We are people who gather to work together to say, "Bless you."' "

"That togetherness is the kernel of quilting. The strange phenomenon about quilting is that it needs to be shared with friends. The sharing of patterns, fabrics, and friendships has been the heart and soul of American quilting since frontier days. Somehow quilting has provided an environment for working together and mutual expression. If you put two quilters in the same room, no matter if they are parents, golfers, church members, or computer operators, they talk about quilts. Hooray for quilting. Hooray for friendships. Hooray for a creative, warm, wonderful way to celebrate them."

Dear Hearts
ORIGINAL APPLIQUÉ DESIGN

Fabric Requirements:
13″ square base block of light fabric
1 or 2 closely coordinated prints for the flowerpot
3 shades of 1 color from a medium-to-dark fabric for the hearts
Embroidery floss

Maureen Walker, who gravitated toward Helen Kelley's charming appliqué friendship block, put her appliqué and embroidery talents to good use in this design, as well as on the Crossroads Quilters block, and on the lettering throughout the friendship quilt.

Unlike cut-out or Hawaiian appliqué, *Dear Hearts* shapes can be arranged freely. The design adapts itself very well to a diagonal 'set,' too.

Place the rim of the flowerpot on top of its base after the base has been appliquéd around its bottom and sides. Arrange the hearts around and on top of the flowerpot and pin in place. After the hearts are appliquéd, draw light lines for the embroidery, which will serve to connect the hearts. Embroider over these lines with the chain or outline stitch (see page 133).

DEAR HEARTS

5 Templates   10 Pieces   Embroidery

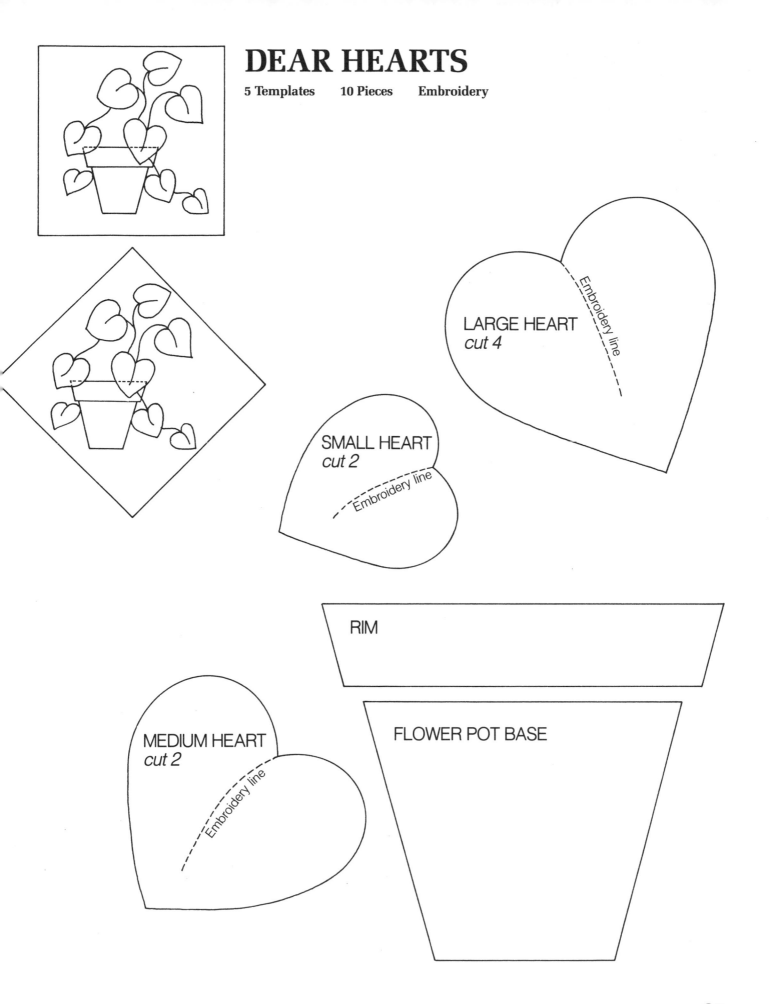

LARGE HEART
cut 4

Embroidery line

SMALL HEART
cut 2

Embroidery line

RIM

MEDIUM HEART
cut 2

Embroidery line

FLOWER POT BASE

Deanne Powell
MELBOURNE, FLORIDA

Deanne Powell began doing needlework when she was still a child. Gradually, her interest in it expanded; she eventually opened a needlework shop and, later, took up quiltmaking. She maintains her dedication to the needle arts as a lecturer for the Embroiderer's Guild of America and has combined her many talents to receive an EGA Teacher's Certification in Quilting. Her special interest in the history of quiltmaking has led her to participate in the Quilt Study Group of Mill Valley, California.

"Quiltmaking has enriched my life with warm feelings and wonderful new friendships. At a time of my life when the children were grown and married, I expected to make few new friends. Quilting was just an interesting hobby until gradually it became an all-consuming pastime and finally a profession.

"The encouragement of many new friends (and of course old friends and family) have brightened each day. Quiltmaking is more than fabric, thread, and needles. It is a blending of our ideas and a sharing of our lives."

Seashell
ORIGINAL PATCHWORK DESIGN

Fabric Requirements:
3 shades of a medium or medium-dark print or plaids, and a light background

The *Seashell*, a Powell trademark, is the symbolic scallop. It was originally composed of 5 radiating triangles set on 2 base pieces (F, E and F, ER). These original 5 triangles have each been divided to provide full-sized templates to accommodate the page size. The templates can be reunited to their original shapes or can be left segmented.

Gwen Wells of Manchester, Massachusetts, another coastal quiltmaker, chose to keep the templates segmented and to alternate a light combination with a dark combination of prints, using her darkest print for the base pieces. The sewing progression is as follows:

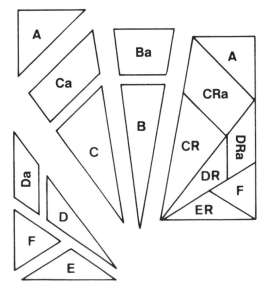

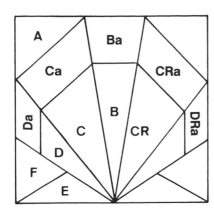

SEASHELL

6 Original Templates or 9 Modified Templates
11 Original Pieces or 16 Modified Pieces

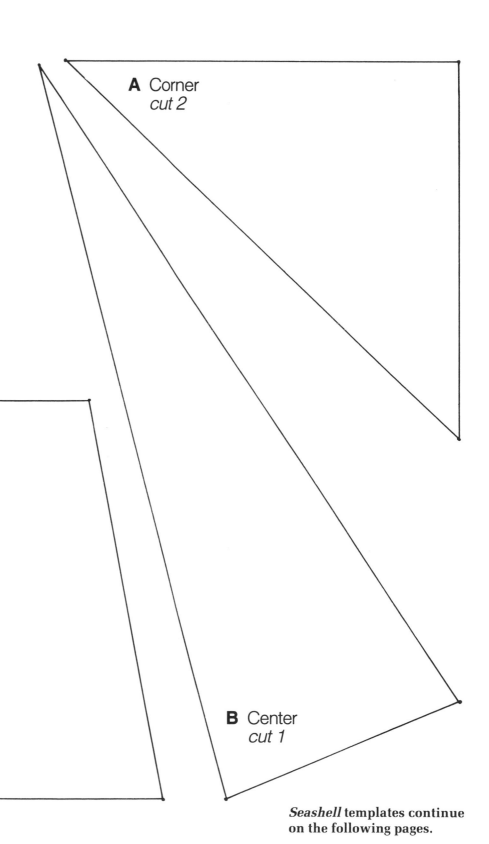

A Corner
cut 2

Ba Center
cut 1

B Center
cut 1

Seashell templates continue
on the following pages.

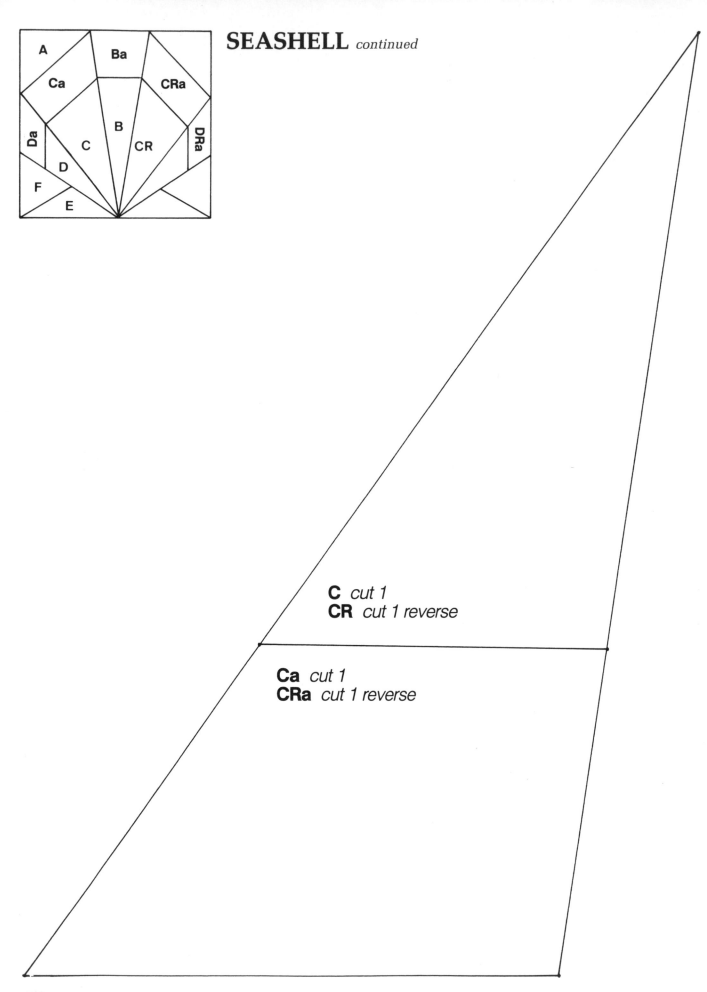

C *cut 1*
CR *cut 1 reverse*

Ca *cut 1*
CRa *cut 1 reverse*

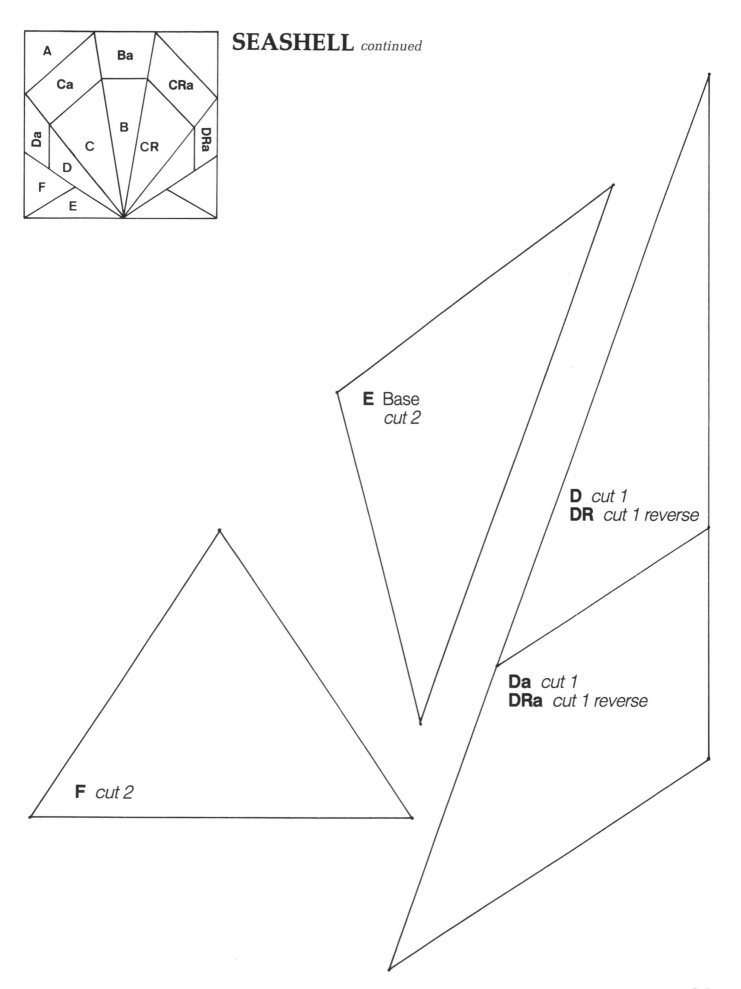

SEASHELL *continued*

E Base
cut 2

D *cut 1*
DR *cut 1 reverse*

Da *cut 1*
DRa *cut 1 reverse*

F *cut 2*

Catherine Anthony

HOUSTON, TEXAS

Catherine Anthony finds both intricate traditional quilts and original contemporary quilts to be a challenge. She is currently at work on a series of contemporary quilts symbolizing individual women whose lives have contributed to the quality of her own. In the quilting field, she is a teacher, lecturer, author, shop proprietor, and a collector of Amish quilts.

"Friendship and sharing are what make quiltmaking different from the other fiber arts. Sharing has been a part of quiltmaking from the very beginning. This has served to enrich the art of quiltmaking as well as the lives of the quiltmakers. May it ever be so."

Rolling Echoes

ORIGINAL PATCHWORK DESIGN

Fabric Requirements:
Lights, mediums, and darks in a wide variety of prints

This is a challenging patchwork pattern designed by a master in pattern drafting for the experienced quiltmaker or adventuresome beginner. Some of the templates are small and some are asymmetrical. The fabric choices are many and will change the emphasis of the design according to their placement; consequently, experiment with many fabrics. Pin all of the fabric choices into their proper place on a piece of paper. After 2 shapes are pieced, pin them back into place on the paper before sewing continues. This block takes time, but will reap great rewards.

Deborah Luce of Manchester, Massachusetts, calmly accepted the challenge of arranging colors and fabrics, and pieced *Rolling Echoes* without a complaint. She chose ecology cloth (muslin) for her C pieces, thus reversing the customary light background/dark design of most traditional patchwork. The corner blocks which combine templates A and B into square units can be formed traditionally, template by template, or by the strip-piecing method mentioned on page 96. The sewing progression is as follows:

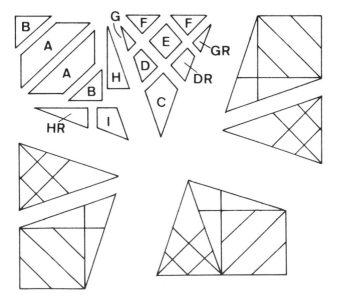

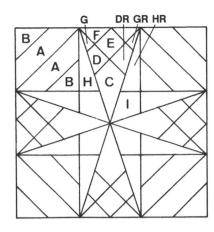

ROLLING ECHOES

9 Templates 60 Pieces

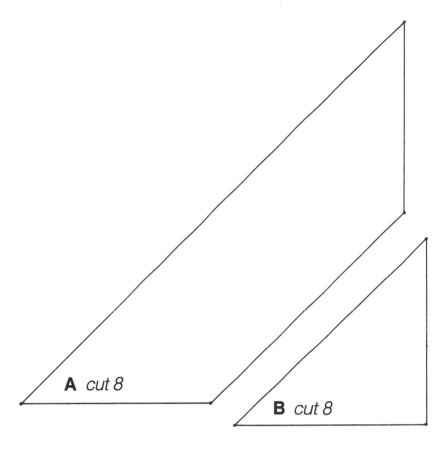

A *cut 8*

B *cut 8*

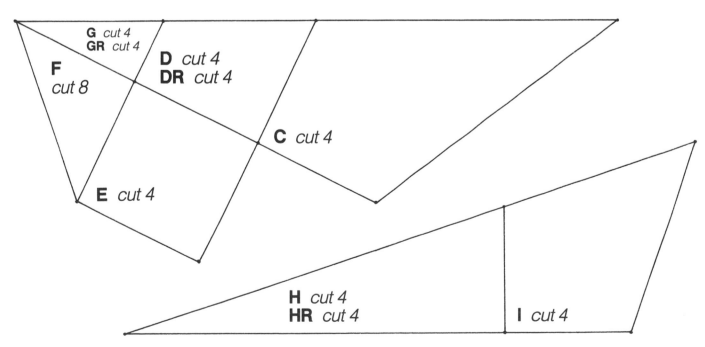

G *cut 4*
GR *cut 4*

F
cut 8

D *cut 4*
DR *cut 4*

C *cut 4*

E *cut 4*

H *cut 4*
HR *cut 4*

I *cut 4*

Libby Lehman
HOUSTON, TEXAS

Libby Lehman is a quilt artist, teacher, and lecturer from Houston, Texas. Married, with 2 children (Les and Catherine), she works from a home studio and specializes in contemporary strip-pieced quilts. Her quilts, all original patterns, have been shown nationwide and are in private collections.

"Twelve years ago, when I first walked into a quilting class, I had no idea my life's work was beginning. What started as "what to do after needlepoint" has become a full-time career in contemporary quiltmaking that is time-consuming, occasionally inspired, intermittently joyous and frustrating, and always fulfilling. Quilting is unique among the arts in that it has a rich tradition of friendship and sharing rather than jealousies and closely guarded secrets. For me, this tradition is vital. I hope that I am giving as much encouragement, friendship, and focus to other quilters as they have given to me!"

Faceted Star
ORIGINAL PATCHWORK DESIGN

Fabric Requirements:
Light, medium, and dark prints in a wide variety of scale

There are definite similarities between *Faceted Star* and *Rolling Echoes* (page 32). Both are stars and have strong diagonal corners; their templates are many, some small and some asymmetrical; and they were created by a talented pair — Catherine Anthony and her daughter, Libby Lehman.

Grace Ladygo of Danvers, Massachusetts, is the junior member of an equally talented mother/daughter team. Greatly influenced by her mother, Gladys Doyle, Grace remembers her mother cautioning her to "make the inside look as well as the outside." That truism definitely applies to the piecing of *Faceted Star*. Small, even seams are a necessity when so many pieces are sewn together. The seams can be kept wide for a sense of security and for easier handling until pieced and then trimmed. Triangular corner tips can be clipped afterwards too. With careful piecing and trimming of bulky seams, *Faceted Star* will lie evenly and be as beautiful from the back as from the front. The sewing progression is as follows:

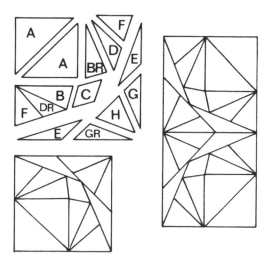

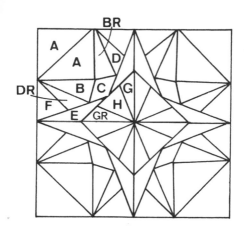

FACETED STAR

9 Templates   56 Pieces

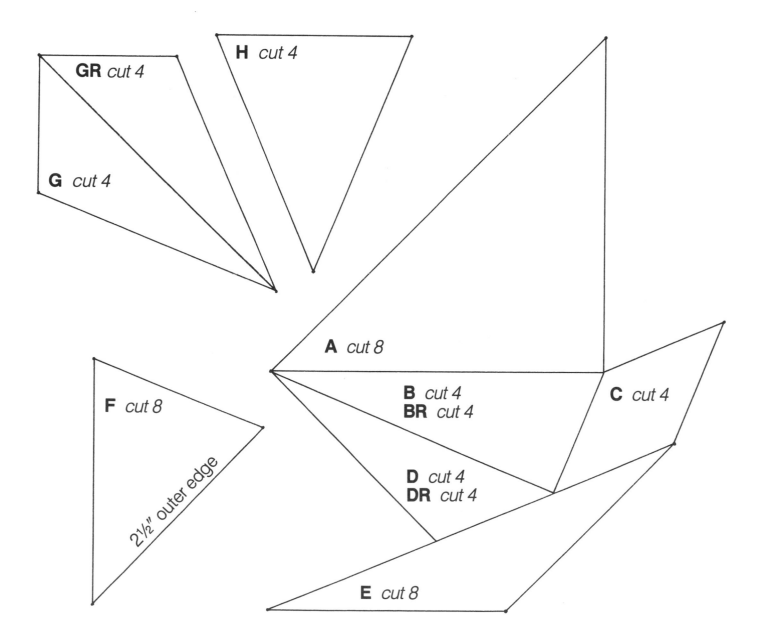

GR *cut 4*

H *cut 4*

G *cut 4*

A *cut 8*

F *cut 8*

2½" outer edge

B *cut 4*
BR *cut 4*

C *cut 4*

D *cut 4*
DR *cut 4*

E *cut 8*

Mary Woodard Davis
SANTA FE, NEW MEXICO

Mary Woodard Davis was born in what is now Oklahoma, and has been interested in fabrics since childhood. Her French and English grandmother was a fine needle-woman, and taught her to sew and embroider before Mary was 6 years old. This art was perfected by the nuns in a convent school where she studied art in all forms, even china painting.

Mary's professional career has included university teaching in Washington, D.C., and in New York City, designing costumes at NBC, and teaching design at Fordham University. In 1959 she moved to Europe and lived with her son in England, and later in Ankara, Turkey, where she spent a great deal of time studying design motifs. While in England she attended several classes at the Royal School of Needlework, studying with such outstanding teachers as Constance Howard, Edith Johns, and Diana Springal.

Since returning to the United States, she has retired to Santa Fe, New Mexico, but continues to share her knowledge as a teacher and designer. In 1969 she organized the Textile Workshops, Incorporated, a non-profit organization devoted to teaching, which features workshops and seminars with internationally known professional textile teachers.

"A memorable recollection of my childhood is the quilt I saw when I was living in Indian Territory, now Oklahoma. It must have been about 1906 or 1907 that I went with my father (who was a lawyer) to visit a Delaware Indian friend of his, George Fall Leaf. The Fall Leafs lived in the country and I don't remember ever being in a house quite like Mrs. Fall Leaf's. There were two rooms: a bedroom and a living room/kitchen. The men did their work in the kitchen while Mrs. Fall Leaf took me to the bedroom. The only thing I remember was a quilt on the bed, blue and white, and she called it 'Cherokee Rose.' It was a beauty, and in my mind's eye I still have an image of that spectacular quilt.

"Quilting has been a continuous interest throughout my life. It was renewed in 1954 by a visit to the Shelburne Museum in Shelburne, Vermont, which has the largest collection of early American quilts in the world. I spent many hours there attending lectures, drawing, and photographing those quilts. When I settled in Santa Fe, I had the chance to unpack many of my quilts that had been stored, and my thoughts turned to 'Cherokee Rose.' I began searching for the pattern. I sent out inquiries over the course of 2 years and received many pictures of quilts by that name, but none matched the quilt of my memory. I finally received a picture that seemed right to me, but I still wasn't sure. I asked my Aunt Clarkie, age 94, about the quilt called 'Cherokee Rose,' and she said she remembered her mother (a Cherokee) having a quilt by that name. Aunt Clarkie asked me to let her sleep on it, and the next morning, she came to breakfast with a drawing of a quilt square, and here it is, my 'Cherokee Rose.' I have worked the design into a contemporary pattern. I have never made it myself, but I will, God willing.

"In 1979 I collected, organized, and exhibited 'The Miniature Fiber: A National Exhibition.' This exhibition was sponsored by the National Endowment for the Arts and the Phillips Petroleum Foundation and traveled for 2 years to 13 locations in the United States.

"In 1980, with the assistance of the National Endowment for the Arts, I collected and exhibited a pictorial quilt show at 10 locations in the United States. In 1982 I made an extensive study of quilt designs, some from as early as the 18th century. Through collectors, museums, and shops I traced a linsey-woolsey design dating from 1790 and another from 1800. I also traced the development and treatment of the 'Wedding Ring' theme and the 'Star' design in quilts made between 1900 and 1982. It was very satisfying to witness this development of design, and the exhibit proved to be a great success."

Fabric Requirements:
13″ square base block of light fabric
1 dark, close print or a solid for stems and leaves*
3 shades of 1 color (print or solid) for petals and flower center
22″ length of ¾″-wide bias for main stem*

*Consult pages 103-104.

Cherokee Rose
ORIGINAL APPLIQUÉ DESIGN

The *Cherokee Rose* is a clear and timeless American design, which appealed to Meg Perkins of Lynnfield, Massachusetts. Note that the quilting design utilizes the appliqué templates and thus is a subtle echo of this lovely pattern.

The first stem to be appliquéd is the longest, with the secondary stems being placed beneath it. Arrange the leaves on top of the stems and then appliqué the leaves. Appliqué the flower, with the left petal slightly overlapping the right petal, then appliqué the heart-shaped petal. Appliqué the center in place, so that it just touches the tip of the heart petal. *These templates do not include seam allowances.*

CHEROKEE ROSE

4 Templates   8 Pieces, plus stems

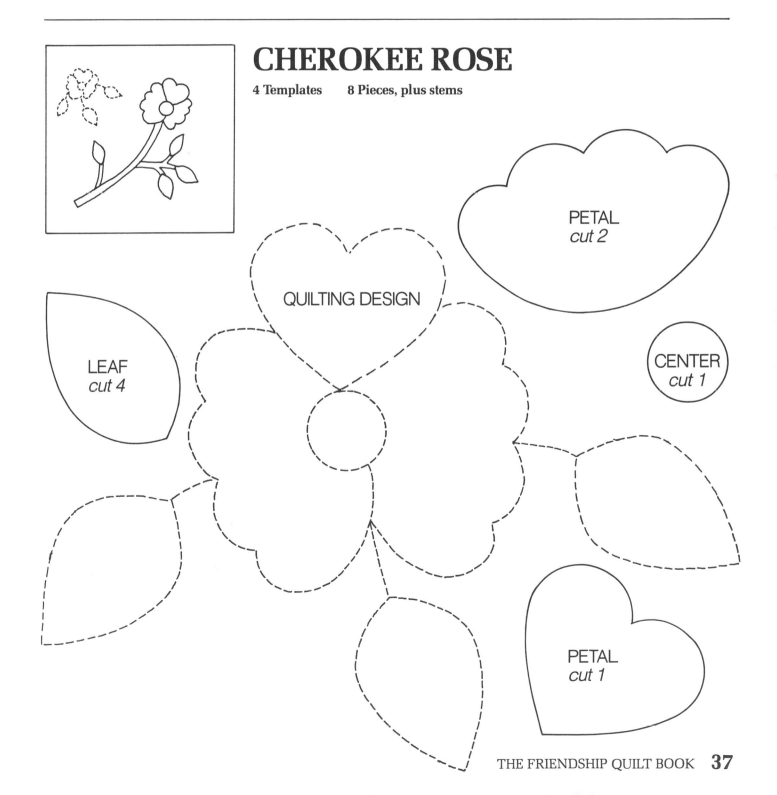

PETAL
cut 2

QUILTING DESIGN

CENTER
cut 1

LEAF
cut 4

PETAL
cut 1

Barbara Brackman
LAWRENCE, KANSAS

Barbara Brackman began making quilts in 1965, when she was in art school at the University of Kansas. Her family, which was originally from New York City, had no heirloom quilts, so she decided to revive what she thought at the time was a lost art. She found Carrie Hall and Rose Kretsinger's book, *The Romance of the Patchwork Quilt in America*, at the library and decided to make a quilt in every single pattern. Since that time, Barbara has abandoned her original goal, but she did try to *index* in her book, *An Encyclopedia to Pieced Quilt Patterns,* all the pieced patterns that have ever been published.

Barbara's quilts have appeared in national publications and exhibits. In addition to writing and lecturing about quilts and their history, she also serves on the board of the American Quilt Study Group and is president of the Kaw Valley Quilters Guild.

"The Ladies Album was a Victorian fad, a place for collecting the contributions of friends — their paintings, verses, locks of hair, and, of course, their autographs, written with a flourish. During the 1840s and 1850s, the Friendship Album inspired a craze for Album Quilts made from friends' contributions. One of the most popular patterns of the time was the Album block. The central cross provided a spot for a carefully inked autograph or one cross-stitched in a fine hand. The pattern, since it was so popular, has come down to us in many variations and with many names, including Chimney Sweep."

Album
TRADITIONAL PATCHWORK DESIGN

Fabric Requirements:
Dark, medium, medium-light, and light prints with 1 fine print or solid suitable for embroidery

Opal Jacobson chose this pattern to piece because she is originally from Lawrence, Kansas, where Barbara Brackman now lives. Following the traditional shading appropriate for an autographed center, Opal chose her darkest fabric for the 4 outer D rectangles while keeping the fifth D rectangle medium-dark for the autograph. (See The Personal Touch, page 131, for autographing instructions.) All of the triangles were kept light for the background and medium-light fabric was used for the 4 center squares (x). The sewing progression is as follows:

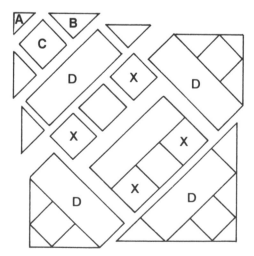

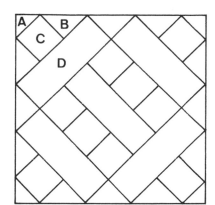

ALBUM

4 Templates   31 Pieces

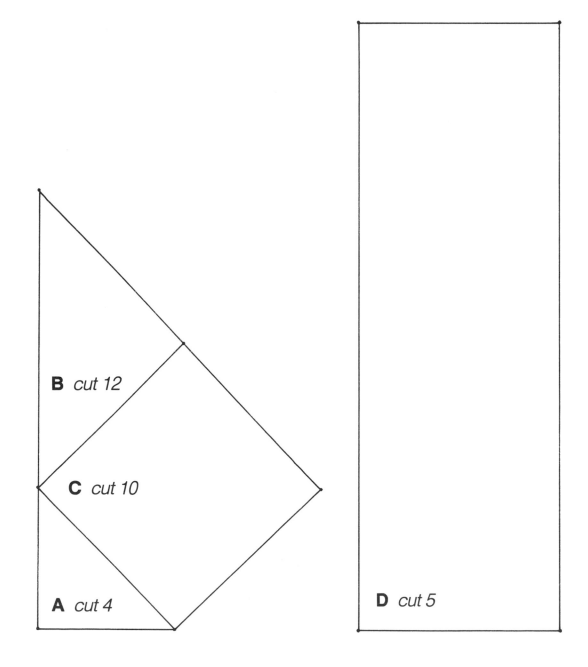

B *cut 12*

C *cut 10*

A *cut 4*

D *cut 5*

Cyrena Persons
MARSHFIELD, VERMONT

Vermont is Cyrena Persons' native state, and the farm is where her life is "at." She and her husband have 6 children. Although home and family keep her busy, she devotes much of her free time to quilting. Cyrena earned her teacher certification in quilting via the Embroiderer's Guild of America in 1980.

"The quilters I know are as warm and comfortable as the quilts they make. I haven't yet met one I didn't like . . . quilt or quilter. These wonderful people have inspired me to greater goals, reassured me in my failures, then praised my efforts. What a boost! These same people have generously shared themselves, be it their successes, their failures, or their dreams. Now, *that's* friendship!

"Quilts have led me along roads I'd never before traveled and to places I'd never seen. The quilters there have made my life happier and fuller. What else could I ask of friendship?"

Farm Life
ORIGINAL PATCHWORK DESIGN

Fabric Requirements:
13" square of background fabric
1 dark, 1 medium, and 1 medium-dark print

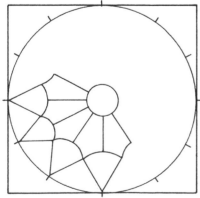

Surely Cyrena Persons and Gloria Webster of Swampscott, Massachusetts, find themselves at home in the center of this design, for the block suggests the complexity of home life. The 12 B shapes revolve around the center A circle like the hours of a clock, and the C shape points radiate to an outer circle like rays of the sun.

Give special consideration to this block by marking notches on templates A, C, D, and E. These notches, marked from the templates onto the fabric, represent the midline of each piece and will be used to ease and distribute fabric evenly around the many curves of the block.

Piecing begins by sewing medium B's to medium-dark B's. Then sew these pairs together until the twelve B's are linked in a chain. Match B seams to A marks and sew the B chain to circle A. When the ends of the chain meet, unite chain B, thus forming a circle. Next, sew D's to one side of the C's, joining them in a similar chain-like fashion. The center C notches will match with the B seams. When pinned in place individually and sewn one curve at a time, they too will form a new circle. The sewing of this circle into the 13" square of fabric can be approached in several ways, but the following method is foolproof. Center and draw a 12" square onto the 13" square of fabric. Then place E in each corner of the drawn 12" square and mark the E curve with notches. A 12" diameter circle is formed by all 4 E's; cut out a smaller circle ¼" in from the E curve line. Now insert the patchwork circle, matching seams with marked notches. Align the grain of circle A with the grain of shapes E before pinning. Move C seams away during this piecing (see flexible seams described on page 94). When each segment is treated (pinned and pieced) separately, the whole circle is not an insurmountable task.

FARM LIFE

5 Templates   **37 Pieces**

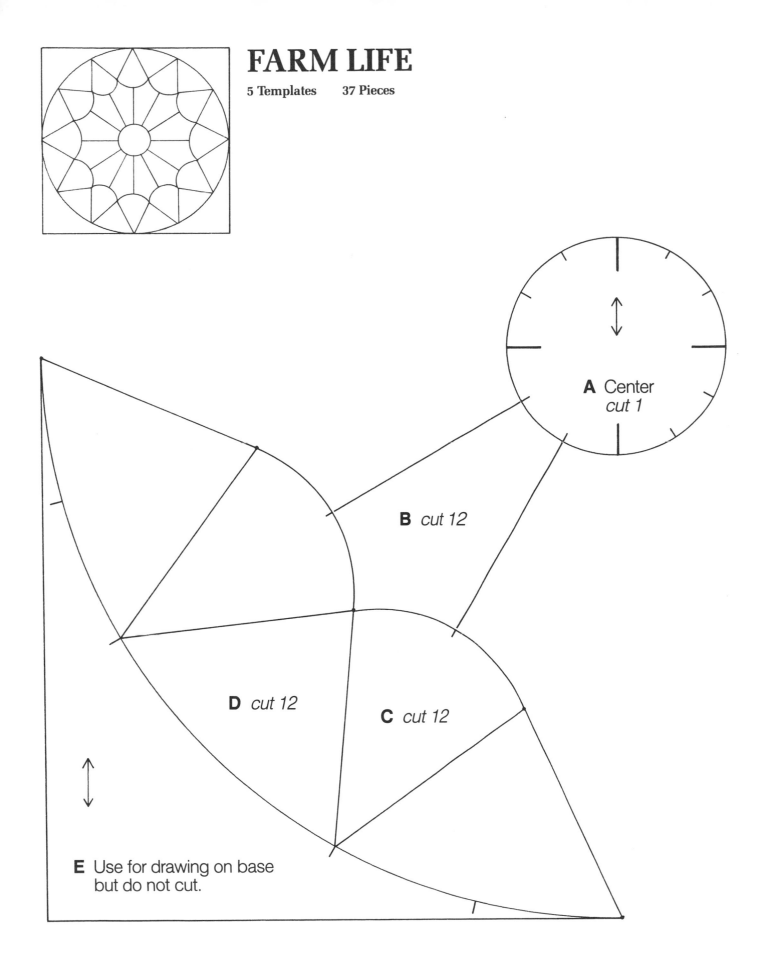

A Center *cut 1*

B *cut 12*

D *cut 12*

C *cut 12*

E Use for drawing on base but do not cut.

Inez Daniel
TENANTS HARBOR, MAINE

Inez Daniel is an energetic great-grandmother; her work outside the home has included nursing, antiques, advertising sales, and owning/operating a general store that sold quilting supplies. She moved to Maine in 1977 and started the Pine Tree Quilters Guild the next year. Today she lives, works, and plays by the sea in Tenants Harbor, Maine.

"I guess this is the first time I've tried to analyze what 'friendship means to me.' As I reminisce about the friends that have shared my life, I realize that they are the people who have shared my highs and lows; have been supportive and constructively critical; and have shared with me their hopes, joys, and concerns.

"Quilting has much in common with friendship. A block, like a person, has its own style, design, color, or personality. It can be pleasing by itself, but when joined in various ways with others, it interacts with surprising, delightful, and often exciting results. Quilting and friends add beauty, texture, solace, and warmth to life."

Storm at Sea
TRADITIONAL PATCHWORK DESIGN

Fabric Requirements:
Lights, mediums, and darks with a possible "isolated" print for the center

A storm at sea may be majestic to the artist but it can terrify a fisherman's family, especially in the winter. This might have been on Roxie Poitras' mind when she chose this block to piece. Formerly from Maine, Roxie remarks that "the earliest American patchwork quilts were made by pioneer women as quickly as possible, so their families wouldn't freeze, and as beautiful as possible, so their hearts wouldn't break." Compare Roxie's shading of this pattern with the traditional shading and then experiment on your own. The sewing progression is as follows:

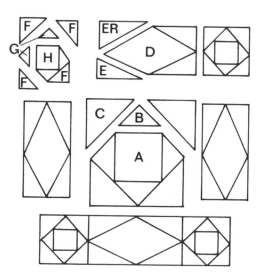

Roxie's shading

Traditional shading

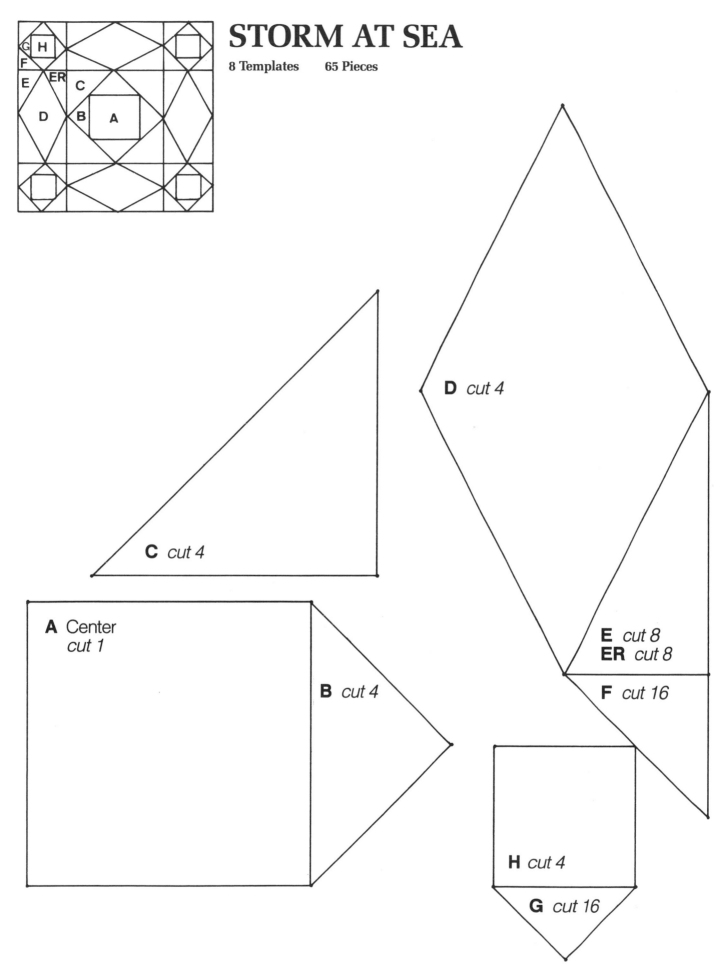

STORM AT SEA

8 Templates   65 Pieces

G H
F
E   ER   C
D   B   A

D *cut 4*

C *cut 4*

A Center
cut 1

B *cut 4*

E *cut 8*
ER *cut 8*
F *cut 16*

H *cut 4*

G *cut 16*

Linda Blair
PETERBOROUGH, NEW HAMPSHIRE

Linda Blair's hillside farm is home to 16 sheep, 2 basset hounds, daughter Anna, son Samuel, husband David, herself, "too many boxes of cloth, and a sewing machine rarely evacuated from the kitchen table in time for supper!" She studied Russian at Radcliffe College and taught Headstart for 8 years before learning to quilt. Soon she was juggling children, creative time, and Joseph's Coat, a unique shop born of Shelley Osborne's love of seamstressing and Linda's love of quilting. Her children sew creatively but, she says, "I have to thread the needles!"

"My life is rich in color, pattern, texture, and awareness of a community transcending distance and time. I read the diary of a colonial quilter and recognize myself in her words. A stranger enters Joseph's Coat. She and I sense kinship and soon baffle bystanders by talking in a foreign tongue, our common language spiced with vibrant quilt names. Her quilts, like mine, have been joint creations — part ours, part history, part inspiration gleaned from a neighbor's sewing basket. We have stitched the same patterns, read the same books, admired the same quilts, shared sore fingers, backache, and the frustration of points that will not meet. We have sewn countless baby, wedding, and friendship quilts, discovering stitch by stitch that art belongs not only to the artistic who can draw (*I* can't!), but to all of us who enrich our lives and celebrate our friendships through needle and thread. We are friends."

Quilter's Mountain
ORIGINAL APPLIQUÉ DESIGN

Fabric Requirements:
13″ square base block
1 light, 2 medium, 2 dark
  prints or solids
Approximately 26″ length of
  2″-wide bias for "Q" circle
  (see page 104 for the
  Modified Celtic Band
  Technique and decide
  whether to use it or the
  traditional approach to the
  bias "Q")

"Q" is for quilter, and within the letter's circular frame a path leads in or out (depending on your point of view), to or from the mountains. Color and fabric choice will alter the effect, especially in the sky area. When choosing a sky fabric, entertain thoughts of dawn with a pastel solid, a winter snow with a small white print on blue, or even a night of navy print. Jane Fulwider, of South Hamilton, Massachusetts, appliquéd this block using a light blue print for a morning sky.

To begin, lightly draw a 7½″-diameter inner circle centered on the right side (as opposed to the wrong side) of the base block fabric. Then draw an 8½″-diameter circle, using the same center point, around the smaller circle. Arrange your fabric choices over the inner circle line, for this will cover seam allowances. Do not, however, allow these fabrics to extend beyond the outer circle line. Position the sky fabric first and baste, then place the left mountain over the right mountain, covering the sky's lower edge completely, and appliqué the upper sides of both mountains. Now place the road on top of the single land piece. Thumb-press, or crease, the end of the road that meets the mountain before folding the end under with the top edge of the land. With this completed, the whole upper edge of land is appliquéd as one unit. Leaving the lower half of the road loose, place the bias around the sketched circle and carefully baste the "Q" in place, with the 2 ends of bias abutting under the road. The ends should not overlap. Before appliquéing the "Q," baste the lower half of the road in place over the "Q" ends, then appliqué the remaining edges.

QUILTER'S MOUNTAIN

6 Templates   **6 Pieces**

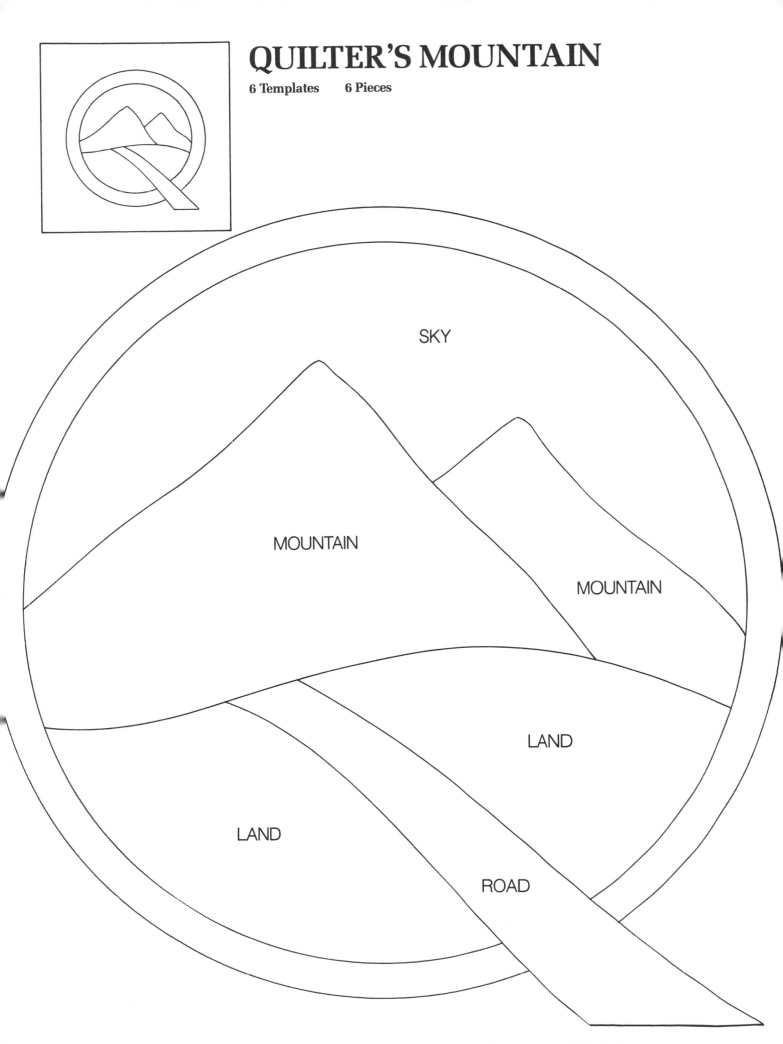

SKY

MOUNTAIN

MOUNTAIN

LAND

LAND

ROAD

Lucy Hilty
BERKELEY, CALIFORNIA

The appliqué quilts of the early 1930s have always been special to Lucy Hilty, who grew up in a Mennonite family in Ohio. Her mother was a quilter and quilting was commonly practiced in the church community. Consequently, Lucy's involvement with this art form began early, during her childhood. Now a retired schoolteacher, Lucy spends her time teaching and lecturing on quilts.

"I really started as a serious quilter when a friend of mine asked me to teach her how to quilt. I found myself thinking about all the things I had known and experienced. Throughout my career as a teacher, each return to my family's home had brought a renewal of contact with quilts and the quilting tradition. Since I've retired from schoolteaching, teaching and lecturing about quilting have led me to a deeper understanding and appreciation of the many values that quilting embodies. My principal interests have become the nature and technique of the quilting stitch and the flow of work that forms the traditional quilting patterns.

"For me, an important aspect of quilting lies in the opportunities for shared work, learning, and achievement. The attraction of quilting extends to all ages, all walks of life. It is an important activity, because it helps me to form friendships with younger people and to break out of the tendency to live in limited contact with only older people. The demands of the work tend to attract people with a common interest and affection for a traditional "women's activity" — younger people who want to explore their heritage and older, experienced quilters who have skills to share. Quilting offers the challenge of craftsmanship and the satisfaction of producing works of lasting beauty and use."

Reel and Sassafras Leaf
ORIGINAL APPLIQUÉ PATTERN

Fabric Requirements:
13″ square base block
1 medium and 1 dark print or
  solid

The Reel pattern appears in traditional appliqué patterns with a thistle and sometimes with an oak leaf. Lucy Hilty designed the *Reel and Sassafras Leaf* and Mary McIntosh of South Hamilton, Massachusetts, appliquéd the block.

As with all symmetrical appliqué blocks, guide creases are made on the base block diagonally, vertically, and horizontally for balance and alignment of pieces. The arc-shaped pieces (B) are lightly creased in half, too. Unfold the leaf shape (A) and match its creases with those on the base block. Place the B pieces on the base block and align their creases with the corresponding horizontal and vertical creases on the base. Position each B piece so that the center point on its inner edge is exactly 2″ from the edge of A (see illustration). Make sure that the ends of the B pieces are far enough under the A piece so that they are completely covered after appliquéing. Baste all shapes, then appliqué the B pieces first, the A piece last. *This appliqué pattern does not include seam allowances.*

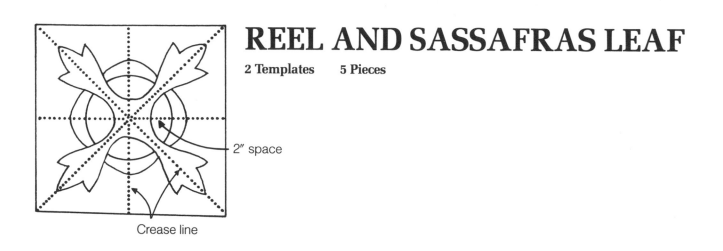

REEL AND SASSAFRAS LEAF

2 Templates   **5 Pieces**

2″ space

Crease line

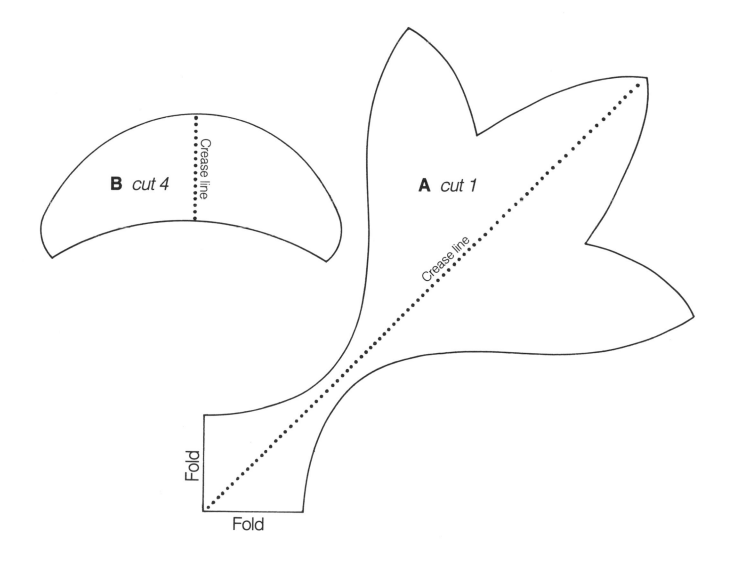

B *cut 4*

Crease line

A *cut 1*

Crease line

Fold

Fold

Margie Boesch

EAST GREENWICH, RHODE ISLAND

Rhode Island winner of the *Good Housekeeping* "Great Quilts of America" contest, Margie Boesch is a quiltmaker, quilting teacher, lecturer, and schoolteacher. Her interests in art, antiques, and sewing led her naturally into quiltmaking. Margie, her husband, and their 2 sons live on a farm in East Greenwich, Rhode Island.

"Making a friend is a lot like making a quilt. We tentatively choose fabrics which will enhance each other; some colorful, some quiet, open weave or closed. After hours of happy companionship, the basic blocks emerge. Some joyfully shout of laughter, some whisper quietly of shared confidences. Love is the thread that holds it all together. Sometimes the thread gets knotted and must be carefully untangled. Even as our lives change and friends drift apart, the quilt remains in our possession. If we have followed the designer's plan, the quilt will be an enduring masterpiece which captures the essence of friendship."

Sunset Star

ORIGINAL PATCHWORK DESIGN

Fabric Requirements:
Light, medium, medium-dark, and dark prints and solids

Susan Grancio, past president of the Crossroads Quilters, arranged many different fabrics before deciding on a combination that highlighted the star. The original design showed corners B/C as divided into 4 segments of equal width (shown on template by dash lines); this is best achieved by strip-piecing. (See page 96 for this special patchwork technique called strip-piecing.) The sewing progression is as follows:

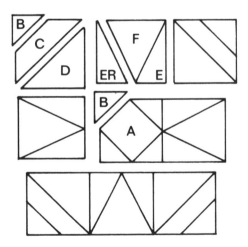

SUNSET STAR

6 Templates **29 Pieces**

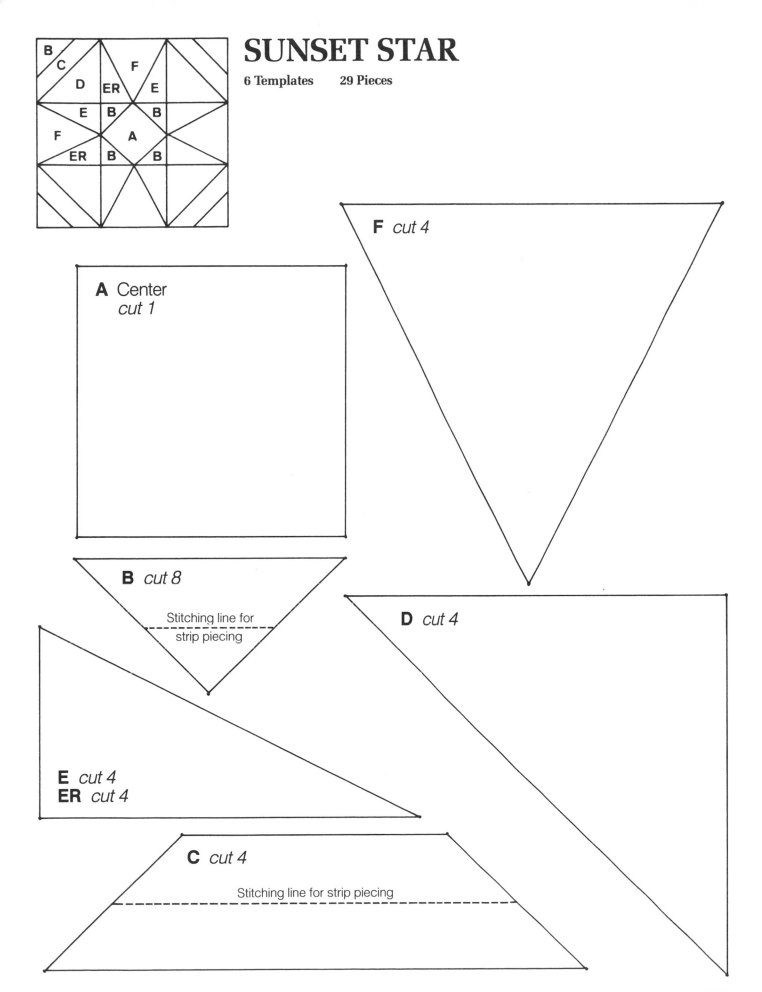

F *cut 4*

A Center
cut 1

B *cut 8*

Stitching line for
strip piecing

D *cut 4*

E *cut 4*
ER *cut 4*

C *cut 4*

Stitching line for strip piecing

Bets Ramsey
CHATTANOOGA, TENNESSEE

Born in Chattanooga, Tennessee, Bets Ramsey is married to poet Paul Ramsey and has 4 grown children. She is an exhibiting artist, a teacher, a writer, and director of the Southern Quilt Symposium.

"I stumbled into the quilt world as a graduate student majoring in textile arts. I discovered a heritage of quilting in my own family which led to further research and documentation of quiltmaking in my region. The people, the stories, and the quilts have become woven into a lustrous tapestry that constantly enriches my life. From my association with the Hunter Museum of Art in Chattanooga, and my work with retired people, I have had the good fortune to know hundreds of quilters from all walks of life. I can't think of a better world."

Double Nine Patch
TRADITIONAL PATCHWORK PATTERN

Fabric Requirements:
1 dark print
Variety of medium prints
1 light background

Bets Ramsey chose the versatile *Double Nine Patch*, noting its endless design possibilities. Kathy Doane of Beverly, Massachusetts, pieced the pattern, and by a "controlled scrapbag arrangement" returned this pattern to its source: the nine patch. Notice that medium and dark prints were concentrated in the corner and center squares and at a distance these squares appear to be the dark squares of the nine patch. The 4 side squares (A) are light for contrast. Within each of the 5 pieced blocks, Kathy put her darkest print in the corners and center, repeating the light/dark arrangement of the simple nine patch pattern. When the pieced squares are arranged with the plain squares, a lovely diagonal chain effect is created, too. The sewing progression is as follows:

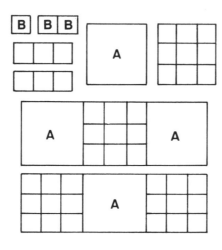

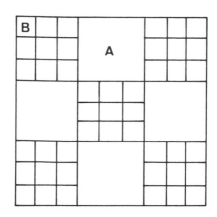

DOUBLE NINE PATCH

2 Templates   49 Pieces

A *cut 4*

B *cut 45*

Vikki Chenette
HARTFORD, CONNECTICUT

Vikki Chenette is an educator and artist with degrees from the University of Bridgeport and the University of Hartford Art School. Her teaching has taken her to schools, colleges, and craft centers throughout New England; her quilts have been exhibited and collected throughout the United States.

"My *Windblown Rose* design is formal and traditional in feeling and I sent it because it refers to love, with the universality of the rose as its symbol. It was created in 1982 for the Old State House's Stately Gardens Exhibit, which was inspired by Hartford's Elizabeth Park Rose Garden. Using this design, I recently made a quilt for a friend far away in New Mexico, in celebration of her daughter's birth. Another version is in Washington, D.C., with an aunt. The title seems appropriate for loved ones far away.

"I have always sought out the community of quiltmakers, and my work has been nourished by the support and interest of friends. As years went by, not all of us continued to make "real" quilts, but we often exchanged blocks or worked on friendship quilts for each other, some using mixed media. The love and generosity expressed in these quilts has always been special. I keep wanting to make quilts that are like bouquets of roses to give away."

Windblown Rose
ORIGINAL PATCHWORK DESIGN

Fabric Requirements:
Light background
3 shades of a medium fabric
2 shades of a dark fabric

Vikki Chenette's delicate 6″ rose design has been repeated 4 times, with each quadrant being given a quarter turn to create the windblown motion. Nancy Anketell, who pieced the pattern, selected 3 shades of a medium color for the rose design and 2 shades of a darker color for the F and H shapes. A medium fabric was alternated with the background fabric in the center triangles, and the light background fabric was again used in the outlying triangles. The sewing progression is as follows:

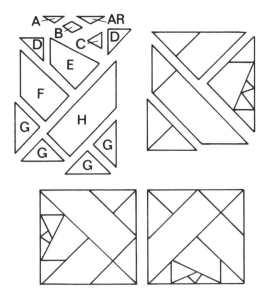

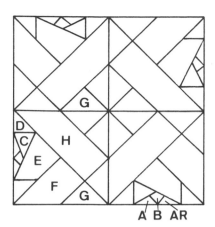

WINDBLOWN ROSE

8 Templates   **52 Pieces**

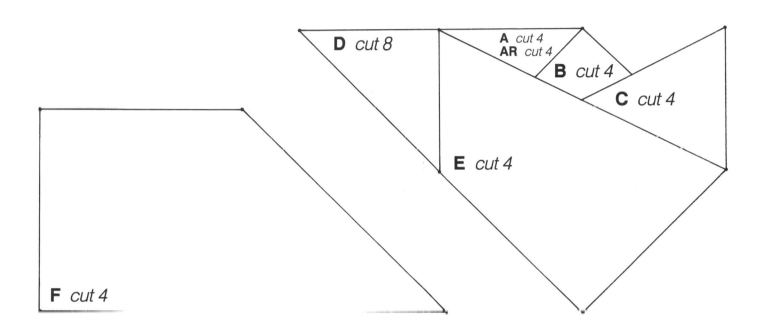

D *cut 8*

A *cut 4*
AR *cut 4*

B *cut 4*

C *cut 4*

E *cut 4*

F *cut 4*

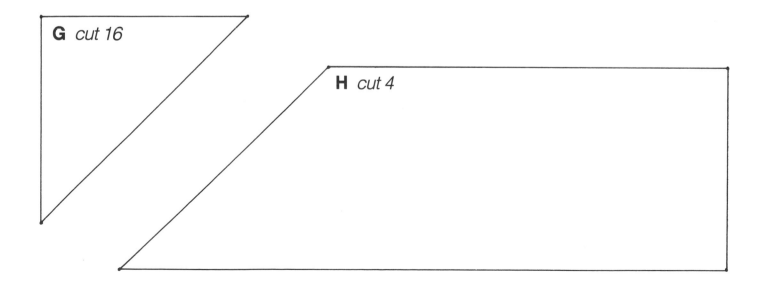

G *cut 16*

H *cut 4*

Vivian Ritter
EVERGREEN, COLORADO

Vivian Ritter knew when she was 6 that she wanted to be a teacher when she grew up, and has fulfilled that dream by teaching English, home economics, and now quiltmaking. As an appreciator and photographer of quilts, she developed several slide programs for The New England Quilters Guild. Vivian particularly enjoys designing children's toys, mobiles, and wall hangings using strip-piecing.

"Images come to mind when I think of what quiltmaking has given me over the years: a wonderful friendship that began when I was spotted in an airport with a *Quilters' Newsletter* under my arm; hours spent in 'quilt-talk' while riding with friends to quilt meetings; a ready-made group of friends when I joined the Colorado state guild after a cross-country move; the continuing link with old friends across the miles, because we still have so much to share. Since quiltmaking is often a solitary effort, the moments spent with friends talking, enjoying, admiring, and dreaming quilts are most precious. Thank you Mary, Linda, Lois . . . ."

Strip Star
ORIGINAL PATCHWORK DESIGN

Fabric Requirements:
Light background
Medium and a close gradation
of 4 medium-to-dark fabrics
Medium-dark or bright print

Vivian Ritter, a master of the art of strip-piecing, has found an alter ego in Susie Astolfi. Susie, knowing Vivian's work with calico in strip-piecing, included a tiny border print as one of the strips and strategically placed it to form an octagonal design. Susie also took the large center square C and subdivided it into strip triangles. (See the discussion of strip-piecing on page 96 before proceeding with this design.) The sewing progression is as follows:

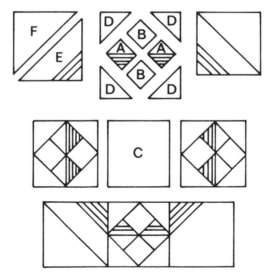

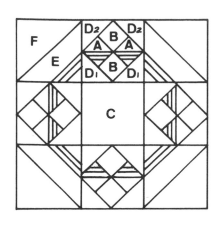

STRIP STAR

6 Templates   **41 Pieces**

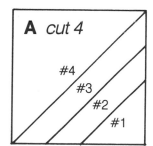

A *cut 4*

#4
#3
#2
#1

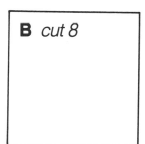

B *cut 8*

F *cut 4*

C Center
cut 1

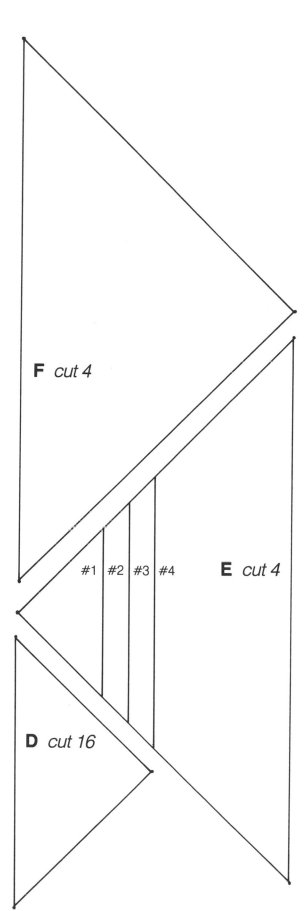

#1 #2 #3 #4

E *cut 4*

D *cut 16*

Mary Golden

NEW HAMPTON, NEW HAMPSHIRE
GLOUCESTER, MASSACHUSETTS

Mary Golden has lived for the past 15 years in New Hampshire (during the school year) and in Massachusetts (during the summer). Twelve of those years have been spent as a quiltmaker, quilt teacher, lecturer, and exhibitor. She has received recognition for her own quilts, for her work with the Kaleidoscope pattern in classes and workshops, and as a charter member and later secretary of The New England Quilters Guild.

"I have discovered a lot about myself and made many friends through quilt-making these past few years. My interests are currently focused on a deceptively simple design, the Kaleidoscope, one with which I feel especially comfortable. The Kaleidoscope and I are better in the company of others or among friends. Alone we both appear rather ordinary, so we reach beyond our borders to form new alliances. We find new vitality, and new vibrant designs emerge.

"Grouped as friends, designs and people work together to create a special energy that quiltmakers so often refer to as 'sharing.' We feel secure almost involuntarily within the group. Our individual talents are realized, and bonds of friendship are developed. We give and receive freely. In groups, designs become quilts, people become friends.

"Quiltmaking will always survive, because we share our talents, our techniques, and our caring. Happy, confident quiltmakers will forever find potential in the individual and in the design beyond the simplicity of its singular form."

Beehive

ORIGINAL PATCHWORK DESIGN

Fabric Requirements:
Light background
Medium-light, medium-dark, and dark prints

The *Beehive* design is a variation of the simple Kaleidoscope design. The 8 large Kaleidoscope triangles have been subdivided into 4 triangles each. This creates the possibility of overlapping four-pointed stars with a careful selection of fabrics. Nancy Whitney of Beverly, Massachusetts, has achieved this effect by her choice of fabrics. The dark four-pointed star rests on the horizontal/vertical axis, and the lighter star rests on the diagonal axis (see photograph of design, page 70). The sewing progression is as follows:

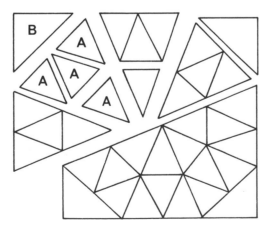

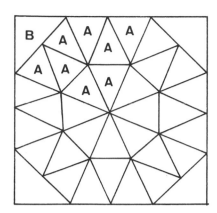

BEEHIVE

2 Templates   36 Pieces

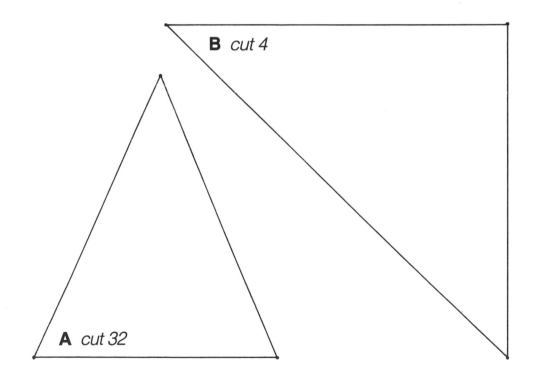

B *cut 4*

A *cut 32*

Crossroads Quilters
WENHAM, MASSACHUSETTS

This 21st design does not appear in the friendship quilt, for it was created as an alternate when one of the 20 block designs had not arrived on deadline day. It can, however, be substituted for any of the other blocks or used as a smaller project, such as the pillow described below.

Crossroads Quilters first met as an organized group in June of 1979. In addition to monthly slide lectures, demonstrations, or workshops, the 75-member group sponsors a series of quilting bees, a supply boutique, and a new lending library. Annual spring quilt shows and pre-holiday fairs provide outlets for members' work and help finance various programs.

Like their quilts, Crossroads members are bound together by strong threads — not only miles of stitches, gallons of coffee, and the electricity of shared ideas, but also countless hours of behind-the-scenes administrative work by volunteers who, like all of us, "would rather be quilting."

Crossroads
ORIGINAL PATCHWORK DESIGN

Fabric Requirements:
Light background
Medium solid or fine print
Medium and dark prints

Pillow Requirements:
16″ pillow form
Two 12″×17″ rectangles
Four 2″×12″ x 16″ mitred
   borders

The shapes of this design converge as the quiltmakers of this group unite. The uninterrupted space of shape A lends itself to a signature, saying, or date which makes this block by itself, in the pillow form, a perfect friendship gift.

Meg Perkins of Lynnfield, Massachusetts, has pieced this block using a medium-colored fine print for shape A, medium and dark prints in shapes B and C respectively, and light background D triangles. Maureen Walker has personalized the block by carefully lettering "Crossroads Quilters" in shape A. (See tips on lettering on page 133.)

After the Crossroads block is pieced and signed, add 2″-wide borders to avoid losing any of the patchwork design to the fullness of the pillow's form. Sew the 12″ lengths of 2 borders onto opposite sides of the finished quilt block; then sew the other two 12″ sides of the borders onto the remaining 2 sides of the block. Finally, sew the mitred corners of the borders from the outer edge inward, ending with reinforced stitches for added strength. Carefully press the patchwork top and borders, and quilt the top, if desired. (See the Quilting chapter, on page 123, for instructions.)

For the back, turn under ¼″ on the 12″ side of each 12″x17″ rectangle and then press; turn under ¼″ again and press; then machine-stitch. Overlap these stitched sides, with right sides up, to form a 17″ square. Center the patchwork top, right side down, onto this and pin. Machine-stitch around all 4 sides, then turn inside out through the back flaps.

*Members of the
Crossroads Quilters Guild.*

CROSSROADS

4 Templates   15 Pieces

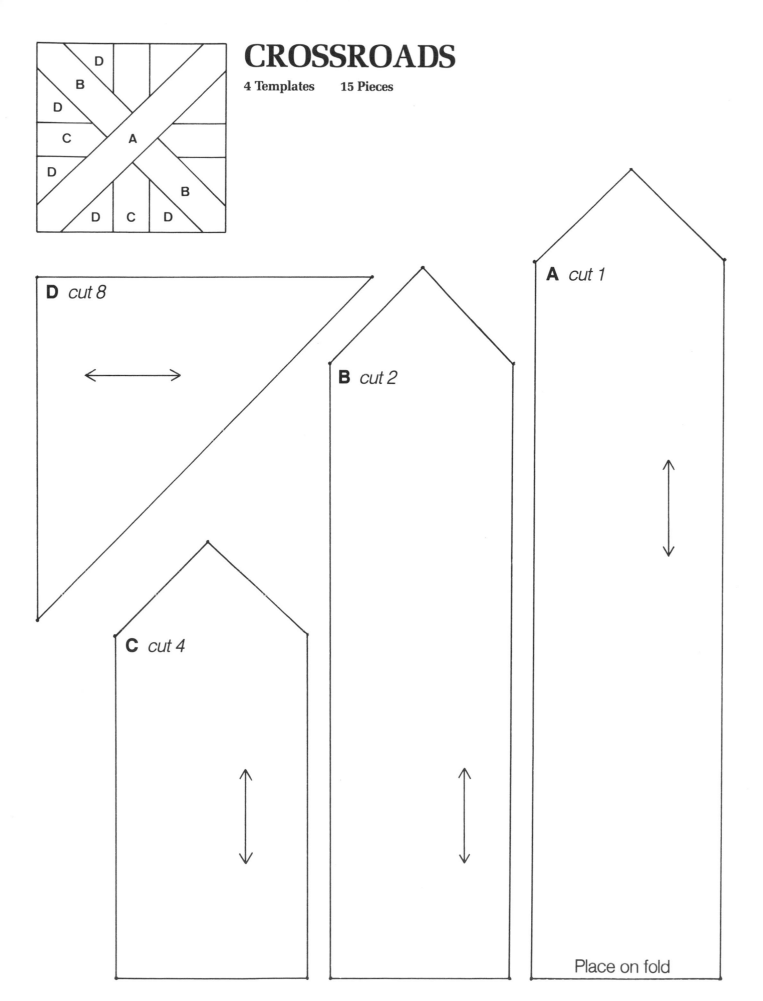

D *cut 8*

B *cut 2*

A *cut 1*

C *cut 4*

Place on fold

A National Friendship Quilt

"This was truly a national quilt project. The book idea was conceived in Sharon, New Hampshire, the designs were sent from all reaches of the United States, and the quilt was begun in Gloucester, Massachusetts, in view of the Atlantic

JOYCE GROSS
MILL VALLEY, CA

LUCY HILTY
BERKELEY, CA

VIVIAN RITTER
EVERGREEN, CO

MARY WOODARD DAVIS
SANTA FE, NM

Ocean. Work on the quilt progressed as the Golden family traveled by car across the country, where, at the home of relatives, the quilt was finished in San Diego, California, on the Pacific Ocean. And, finally, the story of this project, in manuscript form, was completed in the heart of America at my family home in Des Moines, Iowa."

INEZ DANIEL
TENANTS HARBOR, ME

CYRENA PERSONS
MARSHFIELD, VT

LINDA BLAIR
PETERBOROUGH, NH

MARY GOLDEN
NEW HAMPTON, NH
GLOUCESTER, MA

NANCY HALPERN
NATICK, MA

MARGIE BOESCH
EAST GREENWICH, RI

VIKKI CHENETTE
HARTFORD, CT

HELEN KELLEY
MINNEAPOLIS, MN

MONA BARKER
KANSAS CITY, MO

BETTINA HAVIG
COLUMBIA, MO

BARBARA BRACKMAN
LAWRENCE, KN

SUE McCARTER
CHARLOTTE, NC

BETS RAMSEY
CHATTANOOGA, TN

DEANNE POWELL
MELBOURNE, FL

**CATHERINE ANTHONY
LIBBY LEHMAN**
HOUSTON, TX

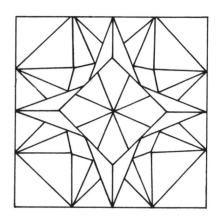

The bird a nest,
the spider a web,
man friendship.

William Blake

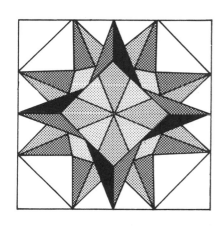

The Color Plates

Quilt Blocks Directory

(See corresponding numbers on pages 66-70.)

PATTERN	DESIGNER	TEMPLATE PAGE
1. ARCHIPELAGO	Nancy Halpern	16
2. BREADFRUIT	Joyce Gross	18
3. COTTAGE STAR	Bettina Havig	20
4. DOUBLE HEARTS	Sue McCarter	22
5. SECRET DRAWER	Mona Barker	24
6. DEAR HEARTS	Helen Kelley	26
7. SEASHELL	Deanne Powell	28
8. ROLLING ECHOES	Catherine Anthony	32
9. FACETED STAR	Libby Lehman	34
10. CHEROKEE ROSE	Mary Woodard Davis	37
11. ALBUM	Barbara Brackman	38
12. FARM LIFE	Cyrena Persons	40
13. STORM AT SEA	Inez Daniel	42
14. QUILTER'S MOUNTAIN	Linda Blair	44
15. REEL AND SASSAFRAS LEAF	Lucy Hilty	46
16. SUNSET STAR	Margie Boesch	48
17. DOUBLE NINE PATCH	Bets Ramsey	50
18. WINDBLOWN ROSE	Vikki Chenette	52
19. STRIP STAR	Vivian Ritter	54
20. BEEHIVE	Mary Golden	56

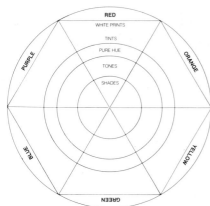

Fabric Color Wheel

This Fabric Color Wheel serves only as an example, for every quiltmaker's wheel will be unique. The objective is not to fill the entire wheel with color, but merely to arrange your fabrics for the purpose of better understanding their relationships with one another and with you. Your own fabric color wheel will be weighted with swatches in your favorite color areas and will reveal those colors with which you feel most comfortable. You'll add more fabrics as your quilt projects increase. A discussion of the Fabric Color Wheel appears on page 78.

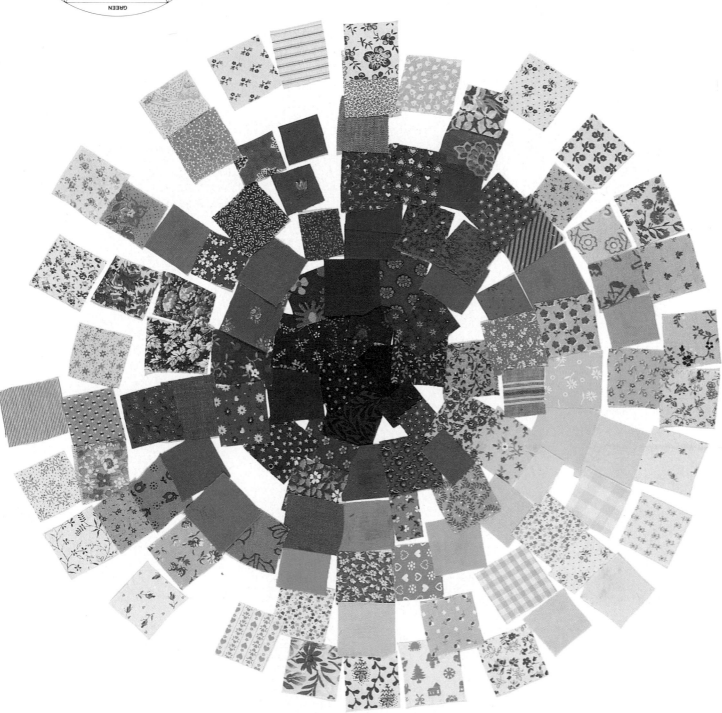

1.

2.

3.

4.

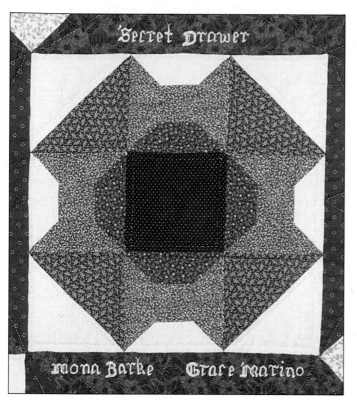

5.

6.

7.

8.

9.

10.

11.

12.

13.

14.

15.

16.

17.

18.

19.

20.

The Quilting Bee

Quilts not only embody creativity, skill, and togetherness, but also provide years of memories and security. Their patterns, quality, and colors are as varied as the people and conditions that create them. Women have always known that quilts warmed spirits and bodies alike and that the natural extension beyond family warmth was friendship's warmth. Women seek companionship, and quiltmaking has provided the common ground.

(Above) *Nancy Anketell, 1984 president of the Crossroads Quilters Guild, concentrates on the fine quilting stitches for the* Star Flower *pattern.*

(Right) *The day-long quilting bee moved quietly into the evening with a dedicated skeleton crew of quilters, who left their family's dinner hour for the companionship of the quilt frame. The author's young daughter, Chassie, and old English Bull Terrier, Hedda Hopper, accompany the quilters with varying degrees of interest. Clockwise from the right are author Mary Golden, Jane Fulwider, and Mary McIntosh.*

The Friendship Quilt

Choosing a Design/ Choosing a Project

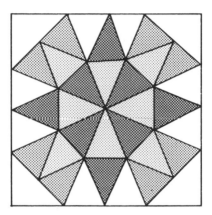

The desire and enthusiasm for creating a friendship quilt are its 2 most essential elements; every other factor emanates from these 2 parts. Where there's desire there's need, and that need dictates a certain kind of organization, which may mean including others in the project or limiting the project size. Time and costs are also important considerations (see the chapter Organizing a Friendship Quilt Project, page 137).

Once you have chosen a block or blocks and a 'set' (an arrangement) for the project, check that the techniques required of the blocks are within your capabilities. If they are not skills that you now possess, spend some extra time on a sample project to develop them (see chapters on Patchwork Designs and Appliqué Designs, pages 89 and 99 respectively). The sample may reveal a hidden ability in that area or may serve to rekindle talent.

Possible Projects

There is beauty in the diversity of patterns in a friendship quilt. Each of the patterns or any combination of them is also a potential quilt. Using only 1 pattern and varying its arrangement, a multitude of possibilities arises for both large and small projects.

After deciding on a project, the next important consideration is the 'set,' which is the arrangement of the block(s).

With the *Beehive* pattern as an example, the following projects are presented.

THE PILLOW PROJECT   A single block with a border as the 'set.' (For complete instructions on making a pillow, see the *Crossroads* pattern on page 58.)

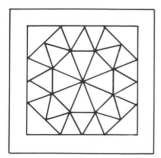

THE WALL QUILT PROJECT Four blocks of 1, 2, or 4 designs with a border and/or sashing as the 'set.'

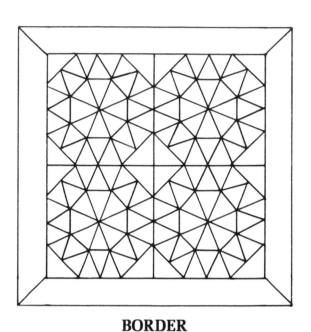

BORDER

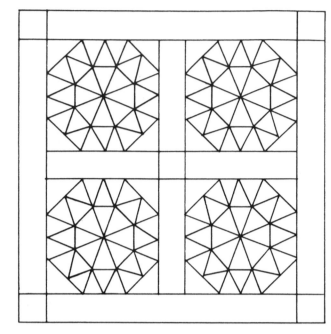

BORDER AND SASHING

For their modest size, quilts have a strong graphic impact on their surroundings. This wall quilt is an arrangement of 4 *Beehive* designs, and the design extends into the simple border. Notice, too, that new designs begin to emerge when 4 blocks are placed together. Altering the fabric choice and color in the center area enriches the whole quilt.

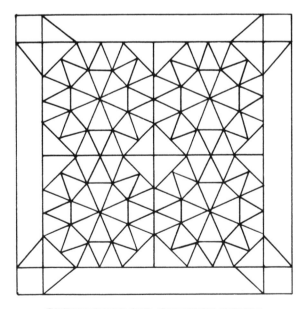

SISTERHOOD OF THE HIVE

THE LARGE WALL OR LAP QUILT PROJECT Five blocks of 1 to 5 designs with a border and alternate plain squares as the 'set.'

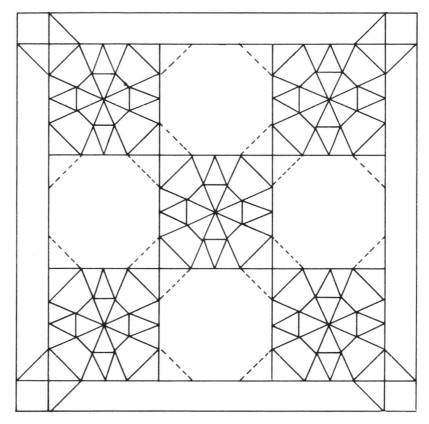

BEE-SPACE

This size is perfect for wall or lap and makes a very special housewarming gift. The arrangement of *Beehive* blocks with plain blocks increases the size of the quilt, but not the time involved. Alternate blocks can remain plain, of course, but lend themselves as well to other patchwork patterns, or possibly to appliqué or quilted blocks.

THE BED QUILT   This is the largest quilt project in the book and contains 20 blocks of 1 to 20 designs; the 'set' is a traditional patchwork pattern called *Idle Moments*.

    The previous examples are merely suggestions, for the possibilities are endless. Although the project size varies, the block size remains 12″ square. The 'set' very often increases the project size without increasing the time. A quilt of 20 blocks does not take 20 times longer to make than a pillow of 1 block. Also, 1 block design used repeatedly, or 4 blocks repeated 5 times, simplifies the project and cuts the time. The same block repeated 20 times can still vary, depending on the choice of fabrics used in each one.

Color Choice/
Fabric Choice

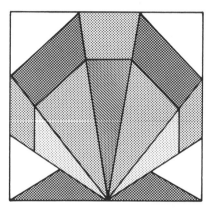

Choosing the colors and fabrics appropriate for a friendship quilt is as important as choosing the designs, the 'set,' and the size of the project, because the completed quilt carries messages with it. In addition to the obvious one of caring, one of the strongest messages comes from the quilt's combination of color and fabric.

To begin with, choose a predominant color for the quilt. This color will be used most frequently and will appear in the quilt's key areas — the primary design in each pattern, the 'set,' and the border. To enhance those key areas, select a secondary color, but use less of it. (Keep in mind that a bright accent color should be used sparingly, and a background color should set the quilt's overall mood.)

Giving plenty of time and careful consideration to color preferences is essential when choosing colors for a friendship quilt project. Ask yourself these questions: Is your favorite color a recent acquisition or a childhood favorite? Will your favorite color be the predominant color in the friendship quilt? Was the color choice a quick decision? Is the color a pure hue or a muted one? Consider the friend receiving the quilt — does a particular color come to mind when you think of your friend? How will the friendship quilt be used? These are all important considerations when determining the final color choice.

Books on color theory rarely discuss the combined emotional impact that color has with fabric. Fabric combines the visual with the tactile, and a quilt is the one very special art form that we can be both physically and emotionally wrapped up in. However, the sheer abundance of fabrics complicates the selection process.

With the current quilt revival now over 10 years old, the resurgence of small-print fabrics has produced prints of every size and color. Border prints, stripes, geometrics, solids and textures, cottons and blends are used both alone and in combination with great daring and sophistication — the available choices are overwhelming. Continued interest in quiltmaking has also fueled a multitude of specialty shops, where, in addition to the large and varied fabric selections, there are also numerous books and patterns that pull quilters' interests in many directions.

A premature trip to the fabric store usually results in one of two reactions. The most common of these is the "I'll-take-one-of-each" reaction; the other is one of complete bewilderment, simply because the choices are too many. A knowledgeable, understanding shop owner may sympathize with your plight and make the decision for you. Anxiety has thereby been relieved, but real choice has been avoided. There are ways to prevent this confusion, however, before you even leave the house.

An at-home search for available fabrics may do nothing more than reveal a favorite color, but even that is helpful. When you place swatches of those fabrics in a small notebook, they begin to take on new meaning. And when you arrange those swatches together in the form of a color wheel (see page 65), even more associations appear. Feel free to use paint swatches and magazine clippings, too, to fill in blank areas on the color wheel.

Color and fabric choices for a group friendship quilt can serve to unify a group. Every fabric purchased has a reason, a story, and memories; an individual's scrapbag or swatchbook can be especially revealing. When a group's fabrics are pooled in the form of a fabric color wheel, a group personality emerges. Personal indecisions are often resolved supportively within the security of the group.

Whether your project is a group or solitary one, color choice precedes fabric choice. Consulting your swatchbook and making a fabric color wheel always precede a trip to the fabric store.

The Fabric Color Wheel

To assemble a fabric color wheel, arrange the 6 basic colors (blue, purple, red, orange, yellow, green) in a circle. The center represents the mixture of all colors and is black. Radiating from the central black area are the shades of each color, gradually lightening to the pure color found midway along each spoke of the wheel. Beyond the midpoints, these pure colors are lightened into tints with grays and, finally, whites. Solid fabrics fill the centermost area of each color spoke, with prints placed to the left or right. Prints include one or more colors and are positioned on the color wheel according to the color that is predominant. A blue geometric design on a red print background is to the left of center and closer to the purple wedge. A multicolored red print with yellow, green, and white flowers may have to be viewed at a distance, squinted at, or considered with eyeglasses momentarily removed to determine this fabric's true colors and eventual placement.

After you have placed fabric swatches on the color wheel, something like a "personal horoscope" of colors emerges. The color wheel will suggest directions and possibilities, as well as points of departure. Some color wedges may be blank while others are filled. Some segments may be filled more heavily above the midpoint of pure hue. A heavy concentration of fabrics in one color segment may suggest a predominant color. Usually, fabrics found at or below the midpoint of each segment are stronger and better possibilities for a predominant color. Perhaps more important than a particular color itself is a predominance in the overall wheel for tint, tone, or shade. If most of the fabrics you have amassed seem to be pastel in all color wedges, they share a common color of light gray or white.

The three terms tint, tone, and shade were merely words applied academically for me until I realized that fabrics of the same value are much easier to coordinate. When a pure color is mixed with white for a tint, it has an affinity with all other colors that have been mixed with white. In the case of a solid fabric, the degree to which it has deviated from its pure color tells me how much of another color was added to that pure color. As for prints, once you have determined the main color, checking the other colors in the fabric will explain in which direction this fabric has departed from its pure color. If you find these terms difficult to assimilate, placing fabrics in the wheel may be your best bet.

The fabrics hardest to place on the wheel will probably be the most versatile, for they represent blends of many colors and they work well with all other fabrics that have those colors in them. Brown does not have its own color segment, for instance, and it may be hard to place. Some browns will have more red in them than others and appear warm. They seem to be comfortable in many locations, but do not fit anywhere in particular. This is because brown is usually formed by more than two other colors and can therefore be used in harmony with almost any other color.

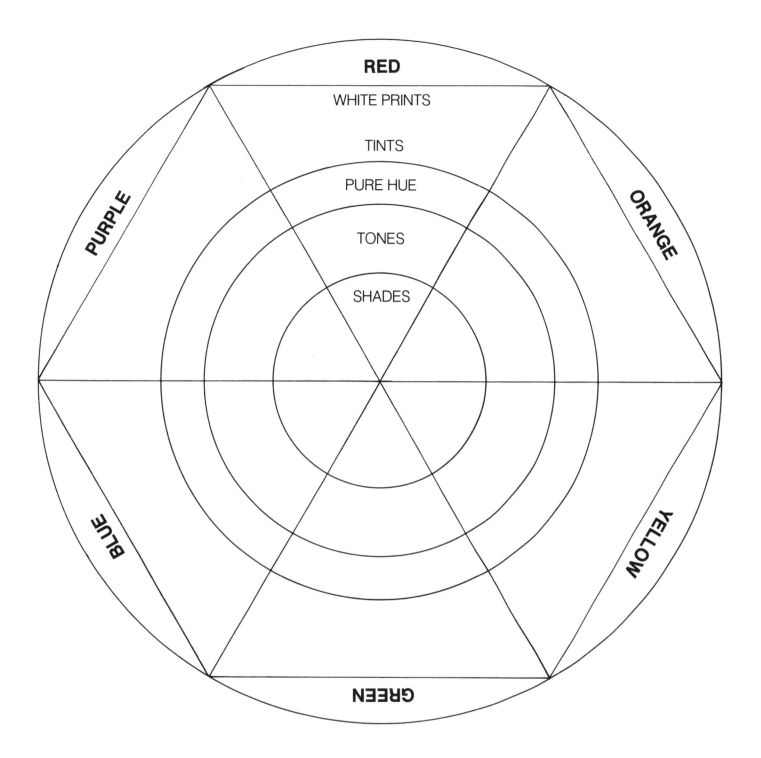

How To Combine Fabrics

The kinds of color schemes and fabric suggestions you draw from the fabric color wheel are an entirely personal matter. You should, however, keep in mind a few basic precepts of color and fabric selection during the process.

When choosing a predominant color fabric and its background fabric color, too, note the contrast between your two choices. Color schemes work well with a lot of contrast as well as with a little, but the degree of contrast may determine your use of prints. Prints tend to soften great contrasts in color and to confuse slight contrasts.

Prints are categorized by scale. The smallest are the calicoes and pin dots; larger ones are referred to as country prints. Some have overall vine-like patterns; others are static with regular repeats. Prints are not static with regard to color, however. They are chameleons, for their colors change with their surroundings and distances.

Prints add a great deal of interest to the fabric surface. They activate, lend depth, and soften edges between different fabric colors, and they can be substituted for solid colors, which can seldom be matched perfectly. White prints are those with colored designs on a white background. The design darkens its light background slightly at a distance, and merges with this background. The more delicate a print, the easier it is to lose. When selecting fabrics, make sure that the prints vary in scale, and include a couple of solid colors as well, for a solid or two will calm a too active fabric surface.

THE GOLDFISH THEORY

Special fabrics, those imbued with their own personalities, very often repel other fabrics, because they demand the spotlight. Unfortunately, these are often the fabrics we choose to be predominant, the very ones that we cherish and gravitate to at the fabric shop. Our sewing shelves may be filled with these treasures.

Conversely, ordinary fabrics — those that are innocuous and even boring — are, like goldfish, often overlooked. They just aren't fabrics that catch our eye. These "goldfish" fabrics are rarely high contrast prints; most often they are grayed, beiged, nondescript fabrics. They may defy placement in the fabric wheel, but this is actually a good sign, since it suggests that they will work well anywhere. The goldfish fabrics will probably prove to be the most versatile of your fabric choices, because they represent a blend of colors.

By the time colors have been considered and the inventory of fabrics arranged, certain characteristics will have emerged to make your fabric color wheel unique. How you will use it and what you decide to take from it become much clearer once you understand the relationships between your fabrics.

Templates

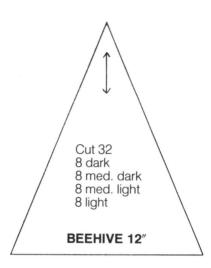

Cut 32
8 dark
8 med. dark
8 med. light
8 light

BEEHIVE 12″

Each pattern in this book is designed within a 12″ square block and each bears a particular name. All patterns, pieced or appliquéd, have several shapes called templates that form the design. Those templates are unique to that block and are shown full-sized unless otherwise noted.

After creating each template, you should label it with the name of the design and the number of pieces to be cut from that template; if there are many pieces, assign a letter to each one and to the corresponding piece on the pattern. All this information serves as a reminder as to where the template belongs. In the case of an asymmetrical template, an "R" designates that the flip side of the template is also to be used.

Since total accuracy begins with precise templates, the way in which the templates are extracted from this book is critical. The material used for the templates is also important, as is finding the method of arranging templates on the fabric that results in the least amount of waste after cutting.

Templates are pattern shapes with points, angles, straight sides, and sometimes curves, all with exact dimensions. The material from which the templates are made must be able to withstand abuse. For example, points must remain points and not be whittled down to rounded edges. Clear plastic is one of the most durable substances, although metal, sandpaper, cardboard, and mat board will also work. The basic rule in determining the template material is this: The more the template is to be used, the sturdier the material should be.

Very often books and magazines will offer full-sized templates, but how the templates are extracted is what determines their accuracy. Pages can be cut out and templates on the page glued to the sandpaper, cardboard, plastic, or other suitable material. The page can also be duplicated. However, the duplication process can distort the template size just enough to cause enormous problems later. Tracing paper can be placed over the page and then onto the template material, but the width of the traced line can also enlarge or reduce the actual size. Finally, there is the push-pin method for extracting patterns, which is recommended for the templates in this book. This is especially useful when templates are contiguous and thus share sides. (See *Windblown Rose*, page 53.)

The Push-Pin Method

When you find an appropriate template material, slip it underneath the pattern for the template, or over the pattern using a transparent material.

Push a pin through the book page onto the material at each corner.

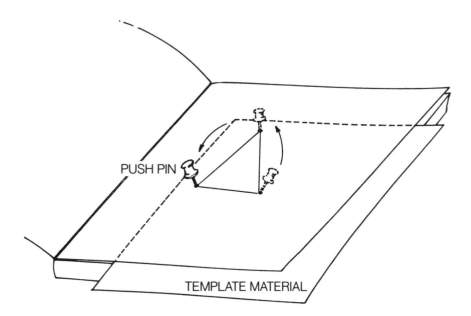

In the case of a curve, make a series of pin points along the curve.

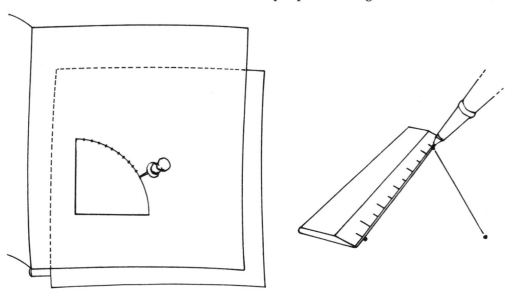

After an adequate number of pin points have been made, remove the template material from underneath the page and connect the dots with a pen and a ruler.

The template can then be cut along the lines with scissors or a mat knife. These will be the most accurate templates possible and will represent the perfect finished shape. They do not, however, include seam allowances. Therefore, when the templates are all cut and ready to be placed on the appropriate fabric, be sure to leave space beyond the template itself for the seam allowances.

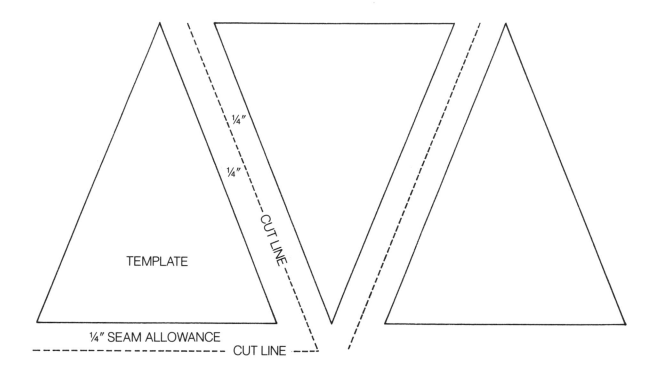

One quarter of an inch is the customary seam allowance used by most quiltmakers, so when 2 templates are set next to one another, two ¼″ seams (or ½″) are required for that space. Some quiltmakers find added security and accuracy in measuring this ½″ width with a ½″ spacer of cardboard; other quiltmakers space by eye. The "by-eye" method of spacing is, of course, not absolutely accurate; but seam allowances do not have to be accurate, only the sewing lines do. A ¼″ seam allowance generally looks too small to a beginning quilter; therefore, "eye-balling" the seam allowance space is the best approach for a beginner, because a wider seam may provide an added sense of security.

Whatever the seam allowance, aim for consistent widths and trim to ¼″ after piecing. Once you begin quilting, you will appreciate why quiltmakers keep the seam allowances small and even. Quilting through extra thicknesses of uneven seam allowances is difficult: it disrupts an even quilting line and adds bulk to the overall quilt.

The Fabric Map

To obtain the greatest number of template shapes from the least amount of fabric, and to lessen the time involved in cutting them, you should first sketch a fabric map. There is no wasted fabric when squares are placed side by side carefully, and there needn't be any when triangles are set together, either.

The fabric map can also be used in determining just how much fabric will be needed for any given template, pattern, or quilt project.

For example, if your project requires fifty 6″ squares, you add two ¼″ seam allowances (½″) plus another ½″ for error, so that the 6″ square will fill a 7″ square area of fabric. If the fabric width is 44″/45″, simply divide the 7″ figure into 44″ (or 45″) and you will find that six 7″ blocks will fit into 1 width with a remainder of 2″ to 3″. Next, if 1 row of width yields six 7″ pieces (6″ squares), and you need 50 of these 7″ pieces, you divide 6 into 50 and find that 8 rows of 6 each are needed, the final row having only two 6″ squares in it. Since our shape was square and filled a 7″ space, 8 rows 7″ wide each will require 56″ of fabric length. Fabric is measured by the yard, so divide 36″ (1 yard) into the 56″ needed, and you get 1 yard plus 20″. The 20″ beyond the yard is figured to the next division of 36″, which is 27″ or ¾ yard. So our final required yardage is 1¾ yards for the fifty 6″ squares. There will be some fabric left over, and some of that amount will be lost to shrinkage.

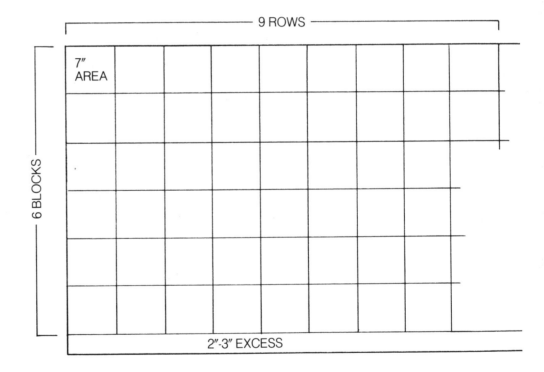

Below are some suggested groupings of the more common template shapes for least waste.

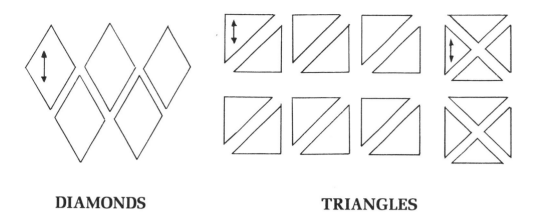

DIAMONDS   **TRIANGLES**

When the template is placed on the fabric for drawing the sewing line, hold the template steadily, and, using a sharpened pencil angled into the side of the template, draw as closely to the template as possible. Corner accuracy is of the greatest importance; draw both sides of corners first, then connect the corners with the side lines.

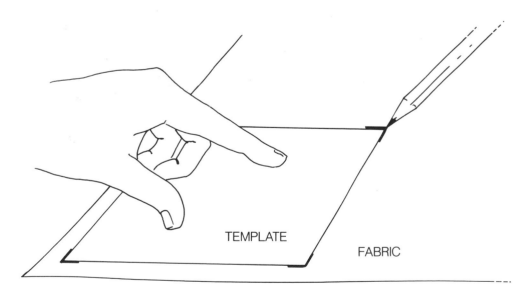

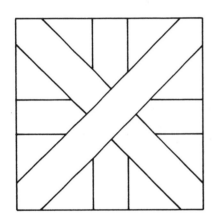

Form ever follows function.
Louis Sullivan, architect

Borders

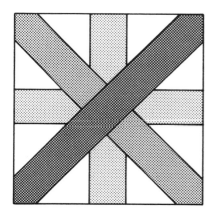

After all of the fabric and supplies have been purchased, prepare the fabric for cutting by washing and ironing it. Because borders generally take up large quantities of uninterrupted length, they should be drawn and cut first, before the smaller pieces eat away at the fabric area.

Borders are usually too long to have templates made for them, but you must measure them as accurately as you would any template. Be suspicious of any and all rulers, and when you do select one, stick with it. Also, be sure to check that wooden rulers have not bowed. Make a square and right triangle templates of cardboard that correspond to the width of your border. Then use these shapes as gauges for drawing corners and consistent widths along the length of the border.

MATERIALS FOR 3″ BORDER

Measure desired border length on fabric with a yardstick.

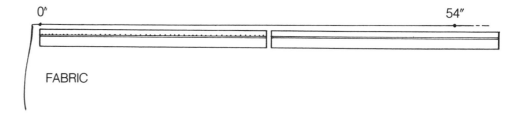

Place the 3″ square on line at point 0″ and 54″ and draw two sides; this will create accurate square angles at the corners.

Place the 3″ square template along the length of the line and mark the 3″ width. Connect these marks to complete the second 54″ side.

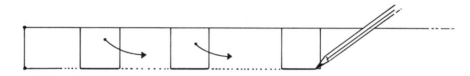

For mitered corners, use the triangle template at each end of the border. The shorter side of the border should correspond to the length of the quilt top.

Patchwork Designs

Hand-Piecing Patchwork

At this beginning stage of quiltmaking, complete accuracy must be stressed. This accuracy is best achieved by using precisely made templates that are carefully drawn around on the fabric. For pieced quilts, the templates are placed and drawn on the wrong side of the fabric. Hand-piecing is done exactly on this drawn sewing line. (See Templates chapter, page 81.) With careful, unhurried piecing comes a finished patchwork block that matches the prescribed size and is square. Inaccuracy, however, results in a block that is too large, too small, puckered, or stretched. Early errors multiply into major problems if not quickly corrected. Inaccurate blocks are difficult to piece together, too, and the frustration of trying to match them leads to a misshapen quilt top. Piecing patchwork is a slow and peaceful procedure. Accuracy and enjoyment almost always occur naturally as a result.

The running stitch is the backbone of all patchwork piecing. No other technique in quiltmaking is so easily learned and so quickly rewarding. This stitch sews 2 pieces of fabric together to form patchwork. The technique never becomes more complicated than that. And when fabric shapes become small or angles acute, it's best to remind yourself that you're just piecing 2 pieces of fabric together from pin to pin at any one time.

Before the needle is threaded and the stitching begins, take time to assemble all of the pieces of the patchwork block you have chosen. Arrange them, right sides up, into the design. This is the perfect time to review your choice of color and fabric placement, for it is much easier to make changes before piecing than after. As a further aid, these pieces can be arranged and pinned onto paper, a square of fabric, or a pillow for easy reference and mobility. Then, when 2 pieces have been sewn together, they can be placed back in the correct position.

Sewing Sequence and Groupings

Now look at your patchwork design and establish a sewing sequence. Generally speaking, small pieces are sewn together early to create larger shapes, with the intention of keeping shapes square and creating rows. As seen in the illustration, the triangles are sewn together first, creating square shapes. Those 3 square shapes are then sewn as a row, and the 3 rows sewn together to complete the finished block.

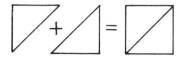

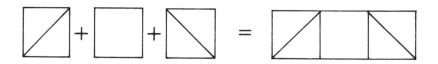

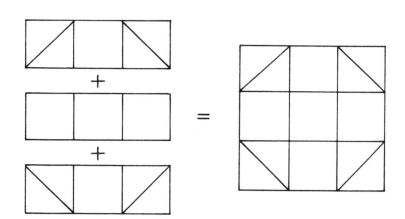

Next, check for similar groupings. If those groupings are sewn at the same time, the repetition creates a more uniform result.

Pinning

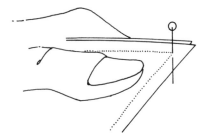

It is now time to pin. Begin by placing the right sides of 2 triangles together, with fingers pinching the side to be sewn as a reminder. Place the first pin through the corner pencil line of the first triangle and into the corner pencil line of the second triangle. Fix this pin perpendicular to the sewing line, in order to allow for proper tension while sewing. The next (and final) pin is set in the same manner.

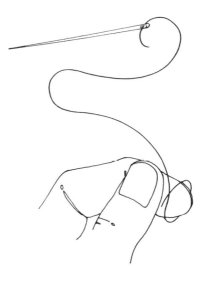

Sewing Thread and Needle

A 12″ length of quilting thread is the strongest and most manageable for piecing. Position this single thread into the eye of the needle, leaving a short tail. You then can knot this length of thread by simply wrapping the end of the thread around your index finger, creating a cross, and then rolling that cross off the finger, forming a small, single knot that you hold while pulling the remaining thread tight.

The needle size depends on the fabric weight and your finger strength. The correct needle is the one that is easy to hold and moves through the fabric thickness easily. Most quiltmakers prefer "Betweens" for piecing and quilting. These needles are short and don't bend; they also have round eyes, which are easy to thread and which can easily accommodate the thickness of quilting thread. This will most likely be the needle that you'll prefer for quilting, too. Learning the quilting technique will be that much easier if the needle is already familiar to you from piecing patchwork.

The First Stitches

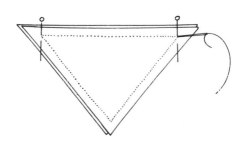

When you have pinned the pieces and threaded your needle, begin the running stitch. Place the needle right through the first pin's hole on the pencil line and fill the needle with 2 or 3 stitches on the drawn sewing line. Before you pull your needle out of the fabric, check that it has sewn through the pencil sewing line on the other piece of fabric, too. Then pull the needle and thread through. As your fingers get stronger and you start to develop a rhythm, your stitches will become uniform and small.

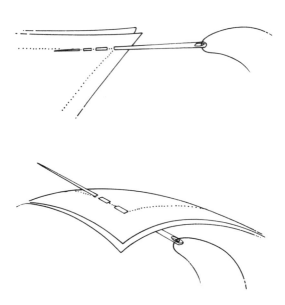

THE ANCHOR Stop for a moment now, and, while still holding the patchwork, position that first pin into a pillow or pants leg for an anchor. This serves as a "third hand," which holds the work in place, while your right hand is free to move the needle through the fabrics. Now, if the 2 pieces being sewn together show signs of not being the same length between the pins, a slight pull of your left hand can equalize the difference.

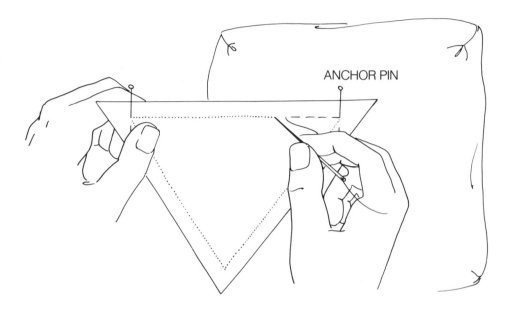

After anchoring the pieces, take 3 or 4 more stitches, check the back piece, pull a little thread through, then repeat this process. Stitch, check, and pull. Keep pulling only a small amount of thread through until the second pin is reached. At this point, pull all of the thread through and take a backstitch. This stitch merely copies the last stitch taken; the needle goes through the fabric a stitch length away from the pin and comes up through the pin's hole. Remove the pins.

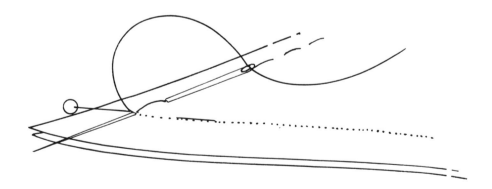

KNOTS AND OTHER PROBLEMS

A knot taken at the end of the sewing line completes the piecing. Wrap the remaining thread around your left hand, forming a loop through which you'll pass the needle. (This loop becomes your knot as you pull the thread tight.) Holding the loop in place on the fabric with your left thumb, bring all the thread through until it is taut and the knot has formed on the fabric.

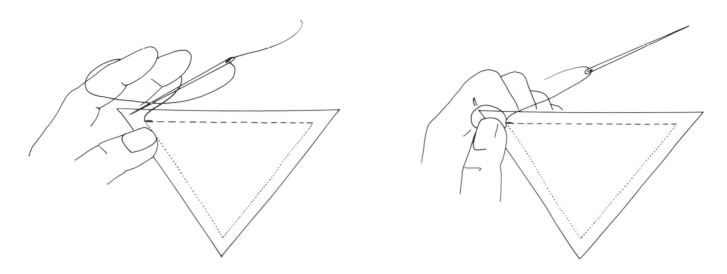

Piecing should be an enjoyable activity — if at any time frustrations occur, don't blame the technique. Sometimes when you are sewing, excess thread will threaten to create an unwanted knot on the sewing line. If this happens, stop sewing immediately. Take the needle and thread in your left hand and put your right index finger into the unwanted loops, straightening them out into just one loop. Keeping that finger in the loop, pull with your left hand until the loop disappears into the sewing line.

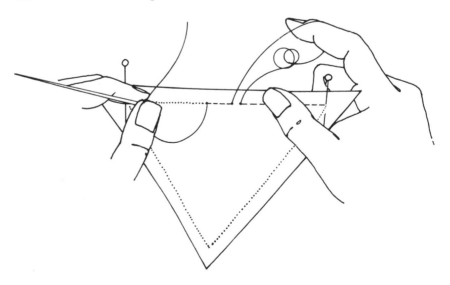

Check your lighting if you start to get a headache. (Bright light is more of a strain than dim light.) Improper seating can lead to stiff shoulders and crossed legs that "fall asleep" from poor circulation.

Once you've worked out all of the kinks, piecing could theoretically continue forever, but try and resist the urge to keep going. To avoid fatigue and other problems, an "activity break" is recommended every hour. This may be the only justification for breaking up an otherwise creative day with errands and housework.

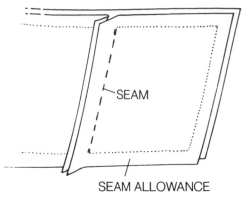

SEAM

SEAM ALLOWANCE

Seams

Piecing with the running stitch never becomes a more difficult matter than the sewing of any 2 pieces together from pin to pin. Seams are created when 2 pieces are sewn together in the process; how you deal with them has a lot to do with the overall accuracy and appearance of the finished patchwork block. There are 2 methods of approaching seams, both of which have merit and can be used interchangeably. The *flexible* seam approach avoids the seam allowance entirely, while the *fixed* seam approach sews them in place.

THE FLEXIBLE SEAM

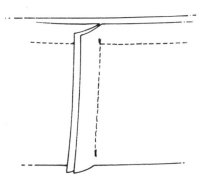

Whenever you are sewing 2 shapes together, and 1 of the shapes has a seam, the running stitch should proceed up to the seam, where you will then take a backstitch. Then move the seam allowance to the right, out of the way of the stitching, and continue the running stitch.

When seams appear and meet on both layers of fabric being pieced, set the pins, as with simple piecing, at the beginning and end of the sewing line (in this case, with all seams moved out of the way). When you reach the second pin, take a backstitch. Leave the needle and thread in place in the fabric, while you reset the pins on the next 2 pieces to be sewn, again moving seam allowances out of the way. As the needle and thread are eased through the seam allowance, they reappear to the left of the allowance. The next stitch to be taken goes into the pin's hole and through the 2 fabrics. A backstitch can be taken here for reinforcement before proceeding along the sewing line.

From the first 2 pieces sewn, through the piecing of shapes into rows, to the completion of the whole quilt top, the above simple principles apply. At any given time, you're just piecing 2 pieces of fabric together from pin to pin.

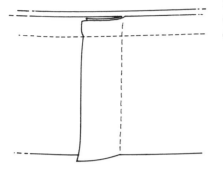

THE FIXED SEAM This approach secures the seam allowance and sews it down in one direction. It is the method most often used on the sewing machine. The trick is to be consistent with the direction of the seam. If fixed seams are later sewn in the opposite direction, the bulking of a crossed seam occurs.

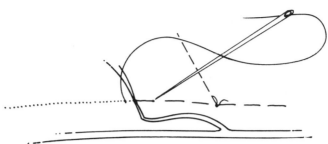

When you encounter a seam along a sewing line, stitch it down in one direction and backstitch it for added strength through the bulk of the seam allowance. If seams appear and meet on the 2 layers of fabric being pieced, you should match them carefully and pin them once onto one of the seam allowances. (Always match the 2 seams in opposite directions to keep bulk at a minimum.) Take backstitches through both seam allowances and proceed to the final pin.

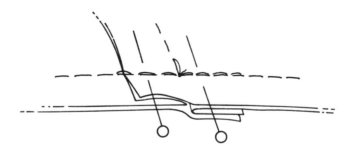

Sometimes the seam allowance pin creates inaccuracy by its angle of placement. This problem can be avoided by guiding the pin into the seam allowance at a 30° angle.

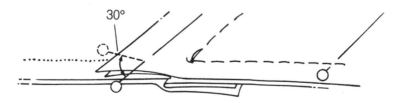

Machine-Piecing Patchwork

People's stitches are a lot like people's personalities — they are both subject to variability. Simply by following basic principles of the running stitch, machine-piecing, like hand-piecing, can result in both accuracy and enjoyment. If you and your sewing machine already enjoy a pleasant relationship, then machine-piecing will also become a pleasant experience. Accurate machine-piecing, though, is a true talent, and there are special considerations to bear in mind. First, piecing begins at the fabrics' edges, *not* at the pinhole. With no knots or backstitching required at the beginning, through seams, or at the end of the sewing line, machine-stitching proceeds nonstop, except to remove pins as you encounter them. A machine stitch set at 10 to the inch and a regular throat plate (as opposed to a zig-zag throat plate) will feed the ¼″ seam allowance through the machine smoothly. Fix pins perpendicular to the penciled sewing line, and pull them out before the needle reaches them. With some patterns, sewing must stop at the pinhole. The needle then stays in the hole as you raise the pressure foot and turn the work around. After lowering the pressure foot again, take a few stitches away from the end. This is a strategic step aimed at strengthening a delicate spot.

Remember, machine-piecing is faster than hand-piecing only when results are accurate and when time is not needed for ripping out mistakes.

Strip-Piecing Patchwork

Strip-piecing adds special interest to patchwork patterns by creating "new fabric" and by further dividing areas in the process. The sewing machine is an indispensable tool in creating strip-pieced fabric. A precise ¼″ seam allowance and careful pressing are also essential. Using Vivian Ritter's *Strip Star* (page 54) as an example, note the 2 areas for strip-piecing, shapes A and E. They can be cut from the same strip-pieced fabric for maximum economy.

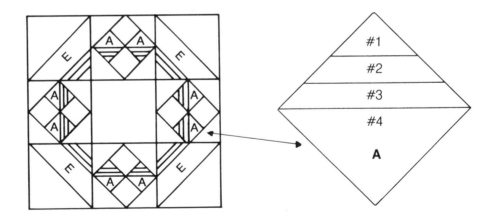

Arrange 4 fabrics in a pleasing color progression and one which corresponds to the numbers from 1 to 4 on shapes A and E. Cut number one 1½" wide, number two and number three ¾" wide, and number four 2" wide, all pieces being 30" long. (These include seam allowance.) Machine-stitch these strips together using a precise ¼" seam allowance. Press all seams in one direction, turn to the right side, then press again, making sure the strips are completely open. Place templates E and A on the wrong side of the strip-pieced fabric, draw the sewing line, and cut a seam allowance beyond. Once cut, these pieces are treated exactly like any other patchwork pieces.

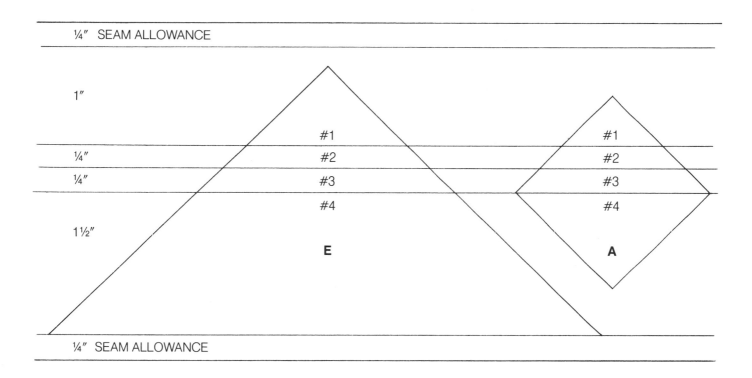

A Reference to Patchwork Designs in this Book

NAME	TEMPLATES	PIECES	PAGE
ARCHIPELAGO Nancy Halpern	7	22	16
COTTAGE STAR Bettina Havig	5	28	20
SECRET DRAWER Mona Barker	4	29	24
SEASHELL Deanne Powell	6 or 9	11 or 16	28
ROLLING ECHOES Catherine Anthony	9	60	32
FACETED STAR Libby Lehman	9	56	34
ALBUM Barbara Brackman	4	31	38
FARM LIFE Cyrena Persons	5	37	40
STORM AT SEA Inez Daniel	8	65	42
SUNSET STAR Margie Boesch	6	29	48
DOUBLE NINE PATCH Bets Ramsey	2	49	50
WINDBLOWN ROSE Vikki Chenette	8	52	52
STRIP STAR Vivian Ritter	6	41	54
BEEHIVE Mary Golden	2	36	56
CROSSROADS Crossroads Quilters	4	15	58

Appliqué Designs

Appliqué

Appliqué, patchwork, and quilting are the 3 staples used in quiltmaking. While patchwork and quilting use 2 forms of the running stitch, appliqué uses a technique called the blind stitch. It, too, is simple to learn and to master, and the method presented here is appropriate for the greatest number of projects. The appliqué blind stitch differs from the patchwork running stitch in that it is worked from the right (as opposed to the wrong) side of the fabric and must be regular, even though the aim is invisibility.

Appliqué differs from patchwork in that the appliqué shapes are usually nongeometric and are layered onto a base block. Some of these shapes require a symmetrical balance, while others are totally abstract in placement. But in all cases, templates for the appliqué shapes are drawn onto the right (as opposed to the wrong) side of the fabric for constant reference.

The Base Block

The base block is the background of the appliqué design and is generally cut from a solid or a fine-print fabric. The base block template for the appliqué designs in this book is a 12″ square made of cardboard or, better still, clear plastic. The base block template is placed on the wrong side of the fabric and sewing lines are drawn around it. Then a generous ½″ seam allowance is cut outside this penciled sewing line. During the appliqué process, the raw edges of the base block may fray or some of the base block's area may be consumed in the stitching process, thus shrinking slightly its overall size. If this happens and the base block has become smaller, place the square template on the wrong side of the base block fabric after it has been pressed and redraw the 12″ square.

SYMMETRICAL APPLIQUÉ Hawaiian, cut-out, and many traditional appliqué patterns require a symmetrical placement of shapes on the base block. This placement is made easier by guide-creasing the base block and the appliqué pieces, then matching these creases (see *Reel and Sassafras Leaf*, page 47).

LAYERING THE SHAPES Many appliqué patterns are created by a build-up of shapes. Flowers and scenes are examples of patterns that require layering. For flowers, the biggest shapes are placed on the base square first, with the smaller shapes placed in order of descending size. Scenes follow the basic rules of perspective. The sky and earth are placed first, with any shapes that appear in front of them following (see *Quilter's Mountain*, page 45).

Sometimes, because of the layering, some shapes need not be completely appliquéd. When one shape overlaps another, the part underneath that does not show is not appliquéd (see *Dear Hearts*, page 27).

PINNING AND BASTING After you have arranged all the shapes, you'll need to pin them for basting. The basting need not be elaborate, but if done correctly, it is a big help in the appliqué process. Baste with a single strand of sewing thread at least ½″ from the raw edge of the shape. Then, as the seam allowance is tucked under ¼″, the basting serves to hold the seam in place while being blind-stitched. Basting any closer than ½″ prevents the full ¼″ seam allowance from being turned under. Basting any deeper than ½″ means that the basting will not help hold the seam allowance under while blind-stitching.

THE BLIND STITCH You are ready to begin the blind stitch when all shapes are basted in place on the base block. Use the same needle as for the patchwork running stitch, but instead of quilting thread, use ordinary sewing thread in a color that corresponds to that of the appliqué shape. (For example, green thread with a green leaf.) Also, keep the thread length to approximately 12″.

Begin on an uncomplicated part of the shape and tuck under the ¼″ seam allowance about an inch at a time, just eliminating the sewing line from view. Holding the base block and appliqué shape in your left hand, push the needle through the back of the base block into and up through the very edge of the appliqué shape. Draw the needle through completely for this first stitch until the thread's knot rests firmly on the back of the base block. The absolutely perfect blind stitch requires that the needle now be placed back into the base block, into the same hole created when the needle pierced the base block in the first stitch. When your needle finds that hole, it takes a stitch on the back of the base block, then comes up again through both the base block and the shape at the same time, just as it did with the very first stitch. Your needle is now on top

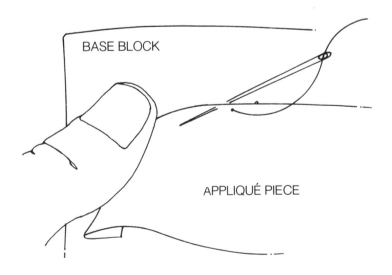

BASE BLOCK

APPLIQUÉ PIECE

and the thread has pierced the shape again. The thread can be drawn through fully again, or, with a little practice at keeping unwanted knots from forming, you need only draw a small portion of the thread through at one time, mimicking the rhythm that develops with the running stitch in patchwork. After 3 or so stitches, very slowly and carefully draw the full thread length through, watching out for forming knots. Depending upon your fabric, the quality of the thread, and your general disposition, you may or may not find that this method works. Some days it does and other days it does "knot."

PROBLEM DAYS On these days, I'm rushed for time and there is pressure to complete projects in a short time span. We all have days like these. However, if there is one key to successful, enjoyable appliqué, it's not to rush yourself. Try not to finish the block at one sitting and you have eliminated the pressure. Just do what you can, then set your work safely aside for a time. Never put your work "away," only aside. Its presence will be a constant reminder, and it will be easier to reach at a moment's notice. When you come to enjoy appliqué, you will want to return to an unfinished appliqué block. There is a bit of a letdown after work is finished, and only the sense of accomplishment puts this feeling aside.

The blind stitch moves along quite smoothly until one or more of the following circumstances occurs:

1. Your straight line curves slightly.

If your seam allowances have been kept to a slight ¼", you will not have to clip along this curve, as even the most careful clips stop the smoothness of the curve and weaken the appliqué. Tuck the seam allowance under with the tip of your needle as you move along and, using the needle, further smooth the seam allowance under evenly to avoid bulking.

2. Your straight line meets an acute outer curve.

Tuck under just enough seam allowance for a stitch or two at a time. Stop forward progress briefly to tuck the full curve under, and distribute the seam allowance evenly underneath. Then, holding this area in place with your left hand, begin to stitch up to and through this area. Do not be afraid to pull the thread through tightly, even to the point of a pucker, so long as you smooth the work out afterwards.

3. Your straight line meets an acute inner curve.

The weakest spot in all appliqué is the "cleft" — where an acute curve changes direction — and this may be the only time to clip. The clip is made perpendicular to and directly into the sewing line. A clip creates a point of weakness, for there is very little, if any, seam allowance up to the clip. So, as the seam allowance decreases, your stitches must become smaller accordingly. This means that at the cleft the stitches are almost on top of one another. Take a stationary (or anchor) stitch right before and after the cleft to reinforce the area. This stitch does not go forward, it overlaps itself. As you begin working away from this point, the seam allowance width increases and your stitches can return to a regular length.

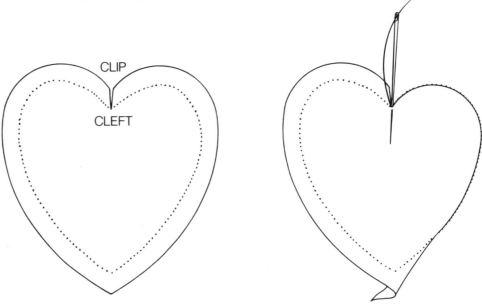

4. Your straight line is approaching a point.

If approached methodically, points present no special problem. This place needs fortification, as some bulking is unavoidable, and any raised surface will wear first. About 1½" away from a point, stop appliquéing and set your needle aside. Clip the tip of the seam allowance off at the point and tuck the remainder directly underneath.

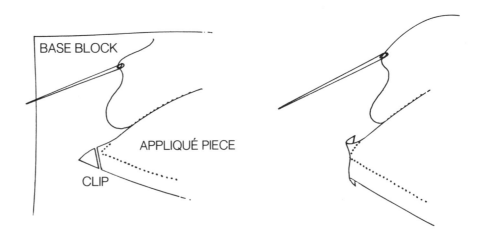

Holding the tucked-under portion with your left thumb and forefinger, begin appliquéing again, using your needle to tuck under the seam allowance up to the point. Then, at the point, take an anchor stitch right into the outermost threads of the fabric. Remember, the anchor stitch has no length — it goes down through the base fabric and up through the hole on the appliqué shape. Pull this stitch snug and turn the work to begin the other side of the point. Some point angles are so acute that only enough seam allowance for 1 stitch can be taken near the point. As stitches progress away from the point, however, a larger portion of the seam allowance can be tucked and thumb-pressed.

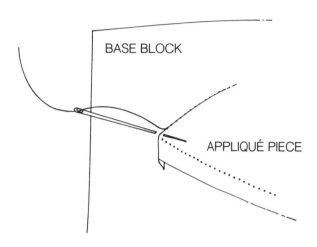

The Heart

The heart shape is a perfect appliqué vehicle for practicing the blind stitch along a gentle curve, into a cleft, and on a point. Use this shape for a small project before attempting a larger appliqué block, for it will sharpen skills and instill confidence. Appliquéd onto a square of fabric, the heart makes a suitable pincushion or miniature pillow project.

Circles, Leaves, and Vines

These shapes deserve special consideration, but not because they are especially difficult. Each in its own way needs to be a consistent shape. Perfect circles, uniform leaf shapes, and regular width vines (and stems) content the eye. Prebasting, normally not suggested, may be exactly what's needed.

In the case of a circle, take a basting stitch in the seam allowance all the way around the circumference. Then place the circle template into the center of the fabric circle and draw the basting up into a pucker that is evenly spaced around the circle. Press, and remove the template.

The leaf shape is generally small, and there is usually more than 1 in a pattern. Prebasting the 2 points and 2 curves reveals the finished leaf shape. Leaves can then be more accurately positioned and carefully angled to the vine.

The width and curve of a vine or stem vary with the needs of the design. The straight of the fabric can be used to make a vine, but only up to a width of ¾″. If it is any wider than this, it won't curve well. The bias, however, can be used under all conditions. In either case, determine the width of the finished vine and cut 3 times that width. For example, ¼″ finished vine width is cut ¾″. (An exception to this is seen in the *Cherokee Rose* pattern on page 37. Here, the bias stem fabric is cut ¾″ wide and folded to a ⅜″ width. The 2 seam allowances are folded underneath, but do not overlap, and form a flat second layer for the stem.) Cut a long template corresponding to the finished width and center it on the wrong side of the vine fabric. Draw lines on both sides of the template. At this stage, you can either press over only 1 side of the vine and appliqué it onto a predrawn curve on the base block, or press under both sides of the vine before appliquéing. Depending upon the fabric, a basting stitch can be taken down the center of the vine to keep it in place before the vine is basted to the base block. Preparing vines in this manner yields a 3-layered appliqué piece that looks a lot like the product of the next approach: The Modified Celtic Band Technique.

THE MODIFIED CELTIC BAND TECHNIQUE

Celtic appliqué designs contain an intricate lacework of bias bands which cover the design pieces. When a large amount of bias is required of a pattern (such as the "Q" in *Quilter's Mountain*, page 44), the stem appliqué approach mentioned earlier may not be adequate. The following is a quick and simplified method of creating (using a sewing machine) a long bias band with a consistent width.

The scene in *Quilter's Mountain* is surrounded by a ½″-wide bias band that is formed into the letter "Q." This band is first cut to 2″x26″, then folded lengthwise with the *wrong sides together*. A seam allowance is machine-sewn a scant ½″ in from the raw edges (or a generous ½″ in from the fold), thus forming a tube with a stitched edge and a folded edge. (The seam allowance may have to be trimmed slightly before pressing the seam to one side to conceal it totally.)

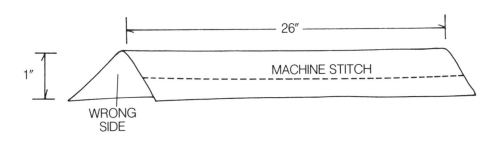

Baste the folded edge of your band onto the outer drawn circle line of the base block, beginning and ending under the tail of the "Q." The central appliqué design has already been stitched in place when the band is basted, and all of its raw edges will fall inside the outer drawn line of the "Q" and underneath the inner edge of the band. When the inner edge of the band is appliquéd in place, and any excess length trimmed under the "Q" tail, the tail is then positioned and appliquéd.

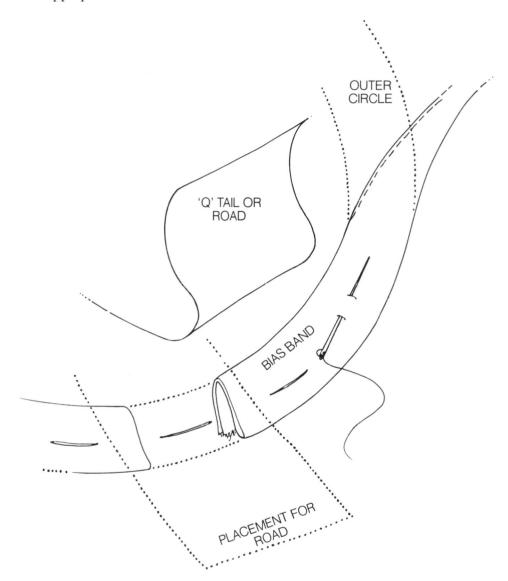

Reverse Appliqué

Reverse appliqué is employed when a shape is so small as to render it nearly impossible to appliqué on top of a surface fabric, as with a bird's eye, for example. The three layers to consider with reverse appliqué are the base block, the appliqué shape, and the scrap pieces of fabric.

As with traditional appliqué, the blind stitch is the stitch to use. Once it is decided when and where to use reverse appliqué, work is no different nor more difficult than other appliqué. The piece of scrap fabric is always larger than the appliquéd opening under which the scrap is intended to go. It need not be any particular shape at first, just larger and consistent in grain.

To reverse appliqué the *Double Hearts* pattern (page 23), make 3 or more cuts into the edges of the heart- and triangle-shaped openings so that ¼″ seam allowance can be turned under as you appliqué around these openings. Center the appliqué shape on guide creases of the base block and pin temporarily. Slip the scrap pieces of fabric between these two layers, positioning them under the heart and triangle openings, and then baste in place.

Appliqué around the inner heart-shaped openings first, remove the basting, fold back the appliqué shape, and trim away the excess from the scrap piece of fabric. (This is an important step because a dark scrap fabric, untrimmed, could appear beneath a lighter appliqué shape as a distraction, and untrimmed scrap fabric might also interfere with other seam allowances nearby.)

Appliqué the triangle-shaped openings next, remove the basting, and trim excess scrap fabric. Then appliqué the outer heart-shaped openings, remove basting, and trim excess fabric. After all the scrap fabrics have been appliquéd and trimmed, appliqué the outside edges of the *Double Hearts* shape onto the base block.

A Reference to Appliqué Designs in This Book

NAME	TEMPLATES	PIECES	PAGE
BREADFRUIT Joyce Gross	1	1	18
DOUBLE HEARTS Sue McCarter	1	13	23
DEAR HEARTS Helen Kelley	5	10	26
CHEROKEE ROSE Mary Woodard Davis	4	8	37
QUILTER'S MOUNTAIN Linda Blair	6	6	44
REEL AND SASSAFRAS LEAF Lucy Hilty	2	5	46

Assembling the Quilt

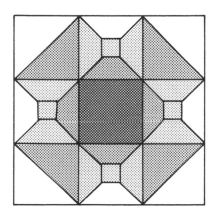

Consider the construction of the quilt top as simply the piecing of one large patchwork block. Don't let the size overwhelm you — if you can piece a patchwork block, then you can piece the quilt top. The following list contains the ingredients of this larger recipe.

The Friendship Quilt

QUILT BLOCKS: 20 friendship blocks, pressed to 12″x12″

'SET' FABRICS: 2 yards light fabric, prepared for 16 C's and 8 A's

2¾ yards medium fabric, prepared for 32 B's
(or 3½ yards for 16)

2¾ yards dark fabric, prepared for 32 D's
(or 3½ yards for 16)

7 yards backing fabric, prepared for 102″x102″ square

OTHER MATERIALS: One 90″x108″ polyester batt
1/2 yard fabric, prepared and cut 1″ wide and 400″ long for bias binding

The Quilt 'Set'

The 'set,' or arrangement, of this friendship quilt is based on a traditional patchwork pattern called *Idle Moments* (see page 76). Here, the blocks are separated by 'set' fabric shapes, which frame each block, as well as impose a strong design that unites the whole quilt surface.

'SET' TEMPLATES

The 'set' templates are divisions and multiples of the basic 12″ square used for the friendship blocks. To create the 'set' templates, simply draw a 12″ square on cardboard, and then draw horizontal, vertical, and diagonal lines through it (see illustration). Cut out the 12″ square and divide it on one diagonal into two 12″ triangles. Arrange these two 12″ triangles in the following ways:

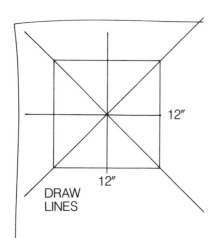

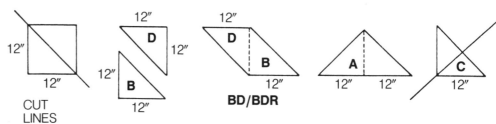

Do not create each template separately, however. Cut the B and D templates first, and use them separately or together to cut the medium and dark 'set' fabrics. Then tape the 2 triangles B and D together to form A. After drawing all of the A shapes on the light fabric, untape template A and cut 1 of the component triangles in half on the drawn line, forming C. Draw C's on the same light fabric as was used for the A's.

Templates B and D — A Special Consideration: BD/BDR

B and D are the two 12″ triangles. When taped together they form parallelogram BD/BDR. How you choose to consider this shape will depend on your fabric's design and will affect the yardage required and the way in which you assemble the quilt top (see illustration).

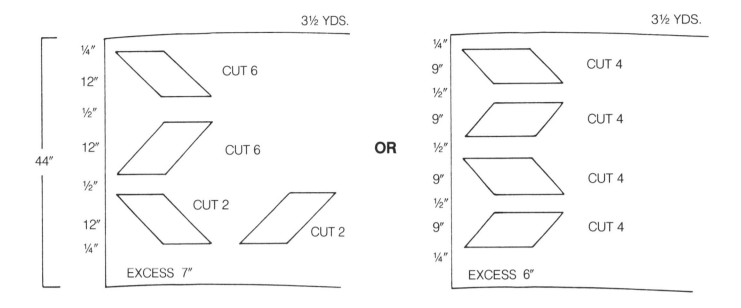

When the medium and/or dark 'set' fabric has a definite pattern, whether striped or floral, consider B and D as one unit: BD/BDR. Watch for subtle pattern directions by unfolding more than a yard of the fabric and viewing it at a distance. When BD is a parallelogram, only 16 pieces are required from each of the two 3½ yards of fabrics, depending upon how BD is placed on the fabrics. BD/BDR is also best used when the quilting pattern chosen would be disrupted by a center seam created when B's and D's are individually cut and pieced. You'll need to make some templates with BD/BDR reversed. Sixteen templates are drawn on each fabric: 8 using one side of the template, 8 using the other (reversed) side. Note this reversal on the template as a constant reminder.

Templates B and D

Templates B and D are the same 12″ triangle. Thirty-two cut B's from the medium fabric and 32 cut D's from the dark fabric are required for the quilt top. By treating B and D as two separate triangles, the template is kept to a smaller size (a 12″ triangle), which is more manageable to draw around and decreases the yardage required to 2¾ yards (see illustration). The piecing of the quilt top appears easier because the rows are straight, but the larger shape (BD/BDR), created when rows are pieced together, will have a center seam. If the center seam does not interfere with the fabric's print or the quilting design, then B and D triangles are recommended.

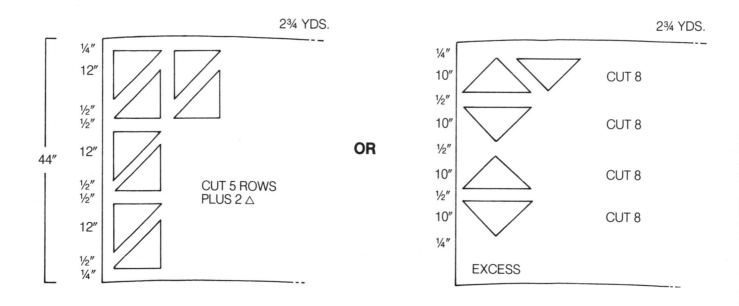

OR

There are 2 ways to place the triangle on the fabric.

In this diagram, the triangle's right-angle corner corresponds with the straight of the fabric, while the long side of the triangle runs along the bias. Biases are notorious for stretching, especially when 2 bias sides are sewn together as in this quilt set.

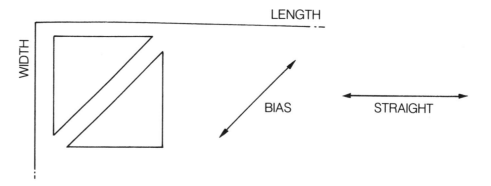

This arrangement places the triangle's long side on the straight of the fabric, reducing possible stretch. If you are machine-piecing the quilt top, this arrangement is definitely the better one.

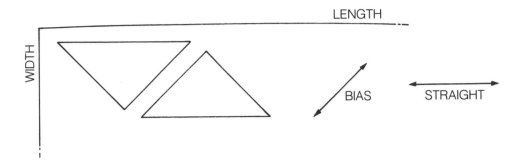

Templates A and C

Cut templates A and C from the same light fabric. Triangle A is a rearrangement of BD.

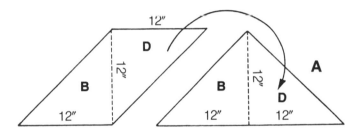

Template C, a 12″ triangle divided in half, is the smallest of the 'set' templates. Draw the A shapes first, then take them apart. Using only one 12″ triangle, divide it on the drawn line. Draw 16 of these C shapes below the larger A triangles on the light fabric.

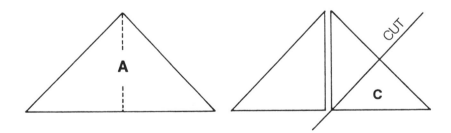

Prepare all 'set' fabrics first by laundering and ironing. Place the templates on 'set' fabrics, allowing for 2 seam allowances between all adjacent pieces and referring to the 'set' diagrams for best use of fabric. 'Set' cutting can occur as an early part of quiltmaking, coming before any friendship blocks are constructed. (In this case, incorporate some leftover 'set' fabrics into the friendship blocks to assure color compatibility.) 'Set' cutting can also occur as the last phase of quiltmaking, when all the friendship blocks have been gathered and the 'set' fabric color choice made as a result of the friendship block colors.

Arranging the Quilt Top

With all of the friendship blocks pressed and 'set' shapes cut, and referring to the quilt illustration (page 76), arrange all of the blocks and shapes row by row on a large bed sheet. The purpose of this arrangement on the sheet is the same as that for patchwork block construction, namely, to check for accurate placement. This is also the time to make any last-minute changes in friendship block placement to achieve a better balance.

Each friendship block design has its own personality, which, when 'set' to color and fabric, becomes something else again. Very often, as with a person, a different side of its personality emerges when viewed in a group setting.

Take a critical look at the arrangement in front of you. Ask yourself these questions: Was your first impression one of delight, or did something bother you? If so, what is the problem? Are your 'set' shape colors overpowering the different blocks, or do they lack needed strength? Is there too much sameness of fabric scale? Is there a good balance between the light, medium, and dark areas? Is the overall effect one of darkness or lightness?

These are horrible prospects to face, especially after time and money have been invested, but it is still better to be honest now. A nagging displeasure with your quilt top at this stage will only serve to slow work through the piecing, quilting, and binding phases, and you will ultimately be left with an unsatisfied feeling. A lot of quilts remain unfinished, simply because the quiltmaker was unable to face changes.

If you sense that the problem is one of balance, make a map of the first arrangement before changing a single block. Move one block at a time and reassess them after each move. Your arrangement may be too top-heavy (that is, some of your darker blocks, or those with large areas of dark fabrics in them, may be too near the top and thus be overpowering). The varying viewpoints of several friends can be an invaluable aid, as long as comments are kept constructive. Without available friends, a Polaroid camera will produce an instant view that can prove very useful.

Sewing the Quilt Top

When many friends have lent their talents to the sewing of the friendship blocks, expect a wide range of ability. Some problems can be avoided by following the basic sewing instructions in the piecing and appliqué chapters. Other problems and their solutions follow.

Blocks are best pressed by one person, all 20 at one time, with a 12″ press sheet of fabric. "Small" 12″ patchwork blocks can be pinned to this sheet and eased to the exact size; "large" 12″ blocks can be pressed carefully into the exact size. When the patchwork block has become larger than 12″ and is being pieced to a 'set' shape, try to absorb the excess length of the block by sticking 2 end pins through the corners of the block and 'set' shape, pinning beyond these pins into the seam allowance. These outer pins then create a tension. The block has a midpoint; match this midpoint with the midpoint of the 'set' shape and see if there is fullness to the left or right. Insert more pins to evenly distribute any fullness you find. If the excess is extreme, you may have to take a seam out of the patchwork block and resew it. The object here is to confine any inaccuracy to the given block and the 'set' shape and not to let the inaccuracy spread.

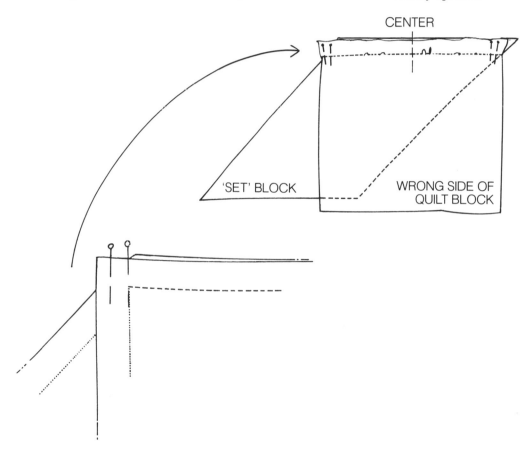

CENTER

'SET' BLOCK

WRONG SIDE OF QUILT BLOCK

SEWING THE QUILT TOP WHEN B AND D ARE SEPARATE TRIANGLES

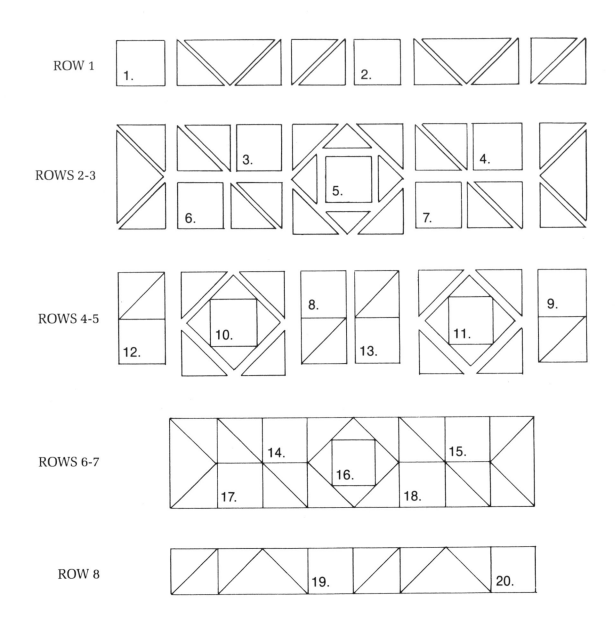

ROW 1

ROWS 2-3

ROWS 4-5

ROWS 6-7

ROW 8

SEWING THE QUILT TOP WHEN B AND D ARE A PARALLELOGRAM

ROWS 1-2

ROWS 3-4

ROWS 5-6

ROWS 7-8

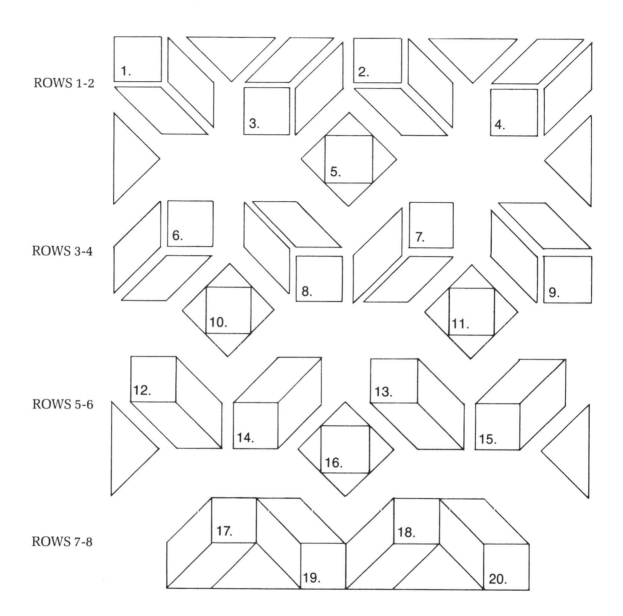

Sandwiching

Why is this quiltmaking process called "sandwiching"? I had originally thought that it referred to the 3 layers — quilt top, batt, and backing — being put together. But now, after having done many sandwichings, I believe the term has an additional meaning and refers also to the fact that the process takes a lot longer than ever expected. In other words, the preparations that began shortly after breakfast have taken you into the afternoon. Sandwiching, therefore, is also a lunch break (!) to replenish your energy, because Sandwiching Day exercises every muscle.

Furniture may need to be moved to expose adequate floor space for quilt assembly, and vacuuming must be especially thorough. The final pressing of the backing and quilt top immediately before assembly also requires special space arrangements. If the "assembly room" is well-traveled, you may need to lock the door to it temporarily or post warning signs. This process is a long, quiet operation for one or a fun activity for two. An extra pair of hands is a lifesaver *and* a kneesaver.

THE BACKING   The backing refers to the back side of the quilt, which is made of fabric pieced together in a size somewhat larger than that of the quilt top. Its color should be compatible with the color scheme of the quilt.

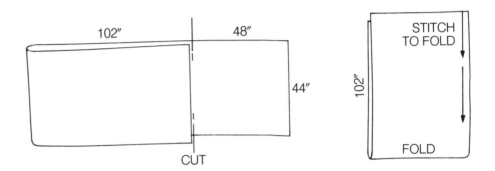

To piece the backing, measure off the first 102″. Fold it, right sides together, over on itself (another 102″) and cut only at the end, leaving the fold intact. Stitch a ½″ seam along 1 selvedge, starting from the 2 cut ends and continuing to the folded end. Now cut on the fold. Clip the very edge of the selvedge off the seam allowance. Open this seam and press.

Take the remaining 48″ length of backing fabric and cut the length into three 15″ strips. Attach these strips along their 15″ sides, yielding a band approximately 132″ long. Press the seams open. With a ½″ seam allowance, sew this band to one of the 102″ sides of backing (right sides together), cut off the excess, and press the seam open. The piecing is now complete.

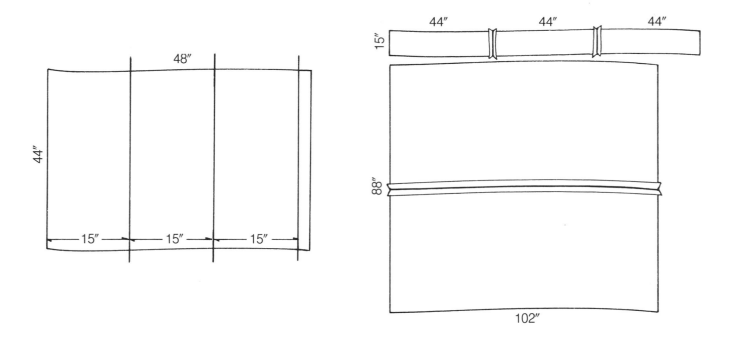

After the laundered, pieced backing has been ironed with the ½″ seams pressed open and selvedges trimmed, place it on top of tables or on the floor with the wrong side up. Tape the backing to the tables or pin it into carpeting at the corners and sides. Avoid stretching it, but do give it a gentle pull to eliminate wrinkles.

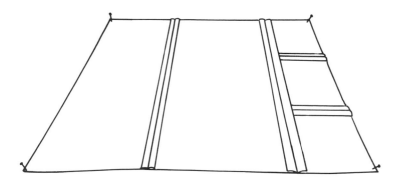

THE BATTING Although batting does exist in a size large enough to accommodate the 96″x96″ friendship quilt, it is generally hard to find. The largest batt stocked in quantity is a generous 90″x108″, which will, when cut and pieced, be adequate. To begin this procedure, gently unfold the batt and place it on top of the backing (which has been secured to a surface to keep it from shifting). Align 1 corner and 2 sides. If necessary, walk over the batt in stocking feet to spread it evenly over the backing, then hook it over the backing pins or tape it to keep it from shifting.

THE QUILT TOP Prepare the quilt top for pressing by first checking seam allowances for evenness. Trim bulky ones and clip the tips off of triangular pieces. Check for loose threads too, then carefully press the quilt top. (Because the pressing requires some time, it is wise to do this a day or so before you plan to assemble the quilt.)

Place the quilt top, right side up, on top of the batt and backing, and position it so that it is 2″ in from their edges. (This allows for expansion or error.) Line up the same corner and 2 sides as you did for the batting. Check that the quilt top and backing are in complete alignment with each other, both horizontally and vertically.

Smooth out the 3 layers in all directions, first from 1 edge and then from the center. This binds them together, and may result in a slight increase in quilt top size. Recheck to make sure that all sides have at least 3″ of excess batt and backing. If your batting measures 90″x108″, some of it will be extending beyond the quilt top, and on another side batt will be absent. Do not cut the batt at this time, however.

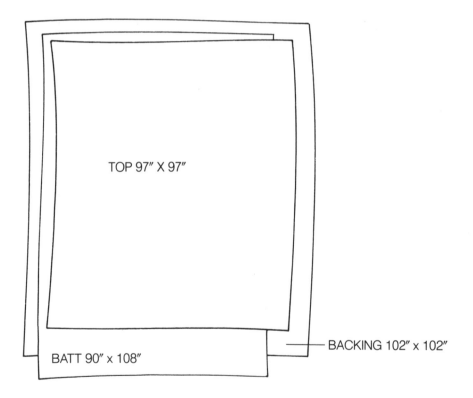

TOP 97″ X 97″

BATT 90″ x 108″

BACKING 102″ x 102″

Pinning

Using straight pins (or safety pins, if children are around), pin the 3 layers together, beginning at the center of the quilt and continuing straight down to the edge; then out from the center and to the left and right. Space pins every 12″ or so. Move yourself around to the opposite side of the quilt, and, keeping the pins parallel to each other at all times, pin from the center down and then from the center to the left and right, gently smoothing as you pin. Pin up to but not to the end of the side that does not have batting.

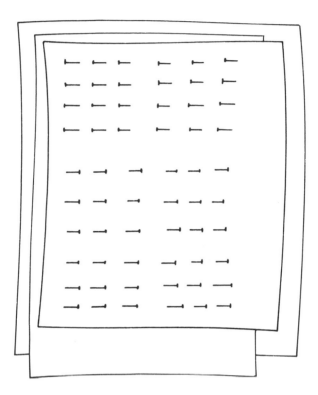

Trim the excess batting from the 1 side. Fold back the quilt top on the absent batt side.

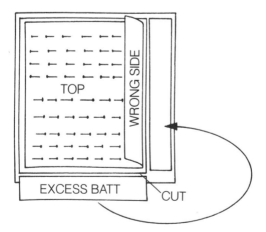

Butt batts against each other and, using a long needle and a long thread, feed the needle horizontally through both batts' edges, pulling gently so as not to create a lump.

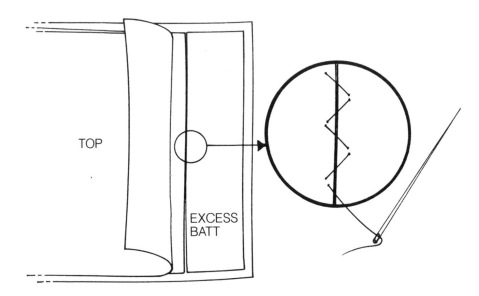

After the batt is pieced, replace the quilt top, smooth out gently, and pin this last section in the same manner as described before.

Basting

A basted quilt is secure yet mobile, for it will weather changes of location and quilting methods. Care taken at the basting stage will insure the quilt's stability.

Basting begins in the center of the quilt and moves to the left. To avoid knotting problems with a long length of thread, thread the needle, but do not cut the thread from the spool. Baste from the center to the left, back-stitch at the edge, then clip the thread. Move yourself to the opposite side of the quilt, and, keeping the spool in the center, baste again in the same fashion from center to left. Repeat for the remaining 2 sides, then baste from the center along the diagonals to each of the 4 corners.

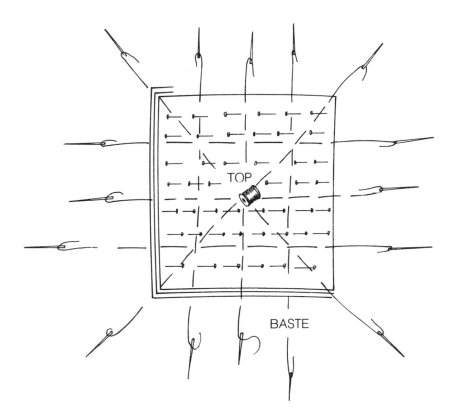

This whole process produces tired knees and a lot of huffing and puffing. Cut the work in half by asking a friend to help. If the pins don't prick you the basting needle probably will, especially if you're talking to your friend. Any spilled blood is best removed immediately with your own saliva.

Once the quilt is thoroughly basted, remove the tape or pins at the edges that have secured it to the tables or floor. Check the back for wrinkles. If you suspect a problem, turn the entire quilt over and pin it to the floor or tables once again. If large wrinkles do not vanish, you have a problem and must remove basting threads in that area and rebaste. This rarely happens, though.

*Trifles make perfection, but
perfection is no trifle.*
By Shaker Hands
by June Sprigg

Quilting

Quilting is the stitched design on a quilt and is best learned by doing. The main objective is to connect the 3 sandwiched layers of the quilt with a needle and thread. This is accomplished by using the running stitch, which was learned and perfected in the hand-piecing process. Every quilter develops an individual style, which comes from hands-on experience. Aim for evenness, which automatically equates with smallness of stitches.

Your first quilting stitches are memorable ones, and what better place to preserve them than on the friendship quilt. They are never to be embarrassed about, for they serve to record where you began and how you improved. Group quilts are known for the variance in ability with regard to the designs, piecing, fabric choice, and quilting. It is the teamwork that is important, not the individual differences.

Quilt Hoops and Frames

Quilt hoops and frames are helpful for 2 major reasons: to insure a flat, smooth, finished quilt with no lumps, and to aid in the quilting process. Quilts can be successfully quilted without these "tools" by using the lap-quilt style, but the need for a hoop or frame increases with the size of the project.

While a hoop isolates a quilt area for an individual's work, a quilt frame stretches the whole quilt on 2 poles and isolates an entire length for several people's work. The sociability of group quilting around a frame is epitomized by the quilting bee. This is still the setting for the all-day-into-evening get-togethers associated with good quilting, good food, good talk, and good friends.

A well-basted friendship quilt project can travel from lap to lap or from hoop to hoop for individual efforts, but nothing compares to gathering around the frame with friends.

Quilting Designs

The quilting on a friendship quilt has traditionally been of 2 kinds. *Outline quilting* highlights each block's design; *'set' quilting* fills the 'set' area with a stitched design that complements the blocks. When the blocks are composed of simple, large shapes, a 'set' quilting pattern is chosen with large shapes also. A similarity in scale adds balance and harmonizes the differences in color, fabric, and design.

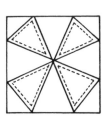

OUTLINE QUILTING

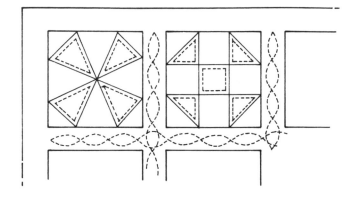

'SET' QUILTING

While the quilting stitch unifies the 3 layers (top, batt, and back), the quilting pattern unifies the surface (blocks and 'set'). The 'set' design itself adds a subtle design to the quilt.

The friendship quilt in this book contains 20 moderate-to-complex patterns 'set' with 12″ triangles arranged to form large parallelograms. These large areas require a quilting design whose shape reflects the scale of the blocks.

Jane Noble's original *Star Flower* quilting pattern was designed with the 20 friendship blocks in mind. Its petal shapes separate the large parallelogram space beautifully and link these areas with the friendship blocks. In addition to unifying the blocks with the 'set,' the petal shapes work with the diagonal seams between colors and avoid the horizontal seams that would have been created if the 2 triangles were pieced to form the parallelogram (see page 114).

STAR FLOWER

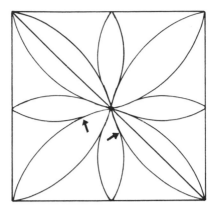

This quilting pattern can be applied to the quilt top before the quilt top assembly or at quilting time. In either case, use white pencil or hard lead pencil to draw around the templates onto the fabric. Draw the large petals first. The small petals are not quilted to the center of the flower but instead begin as outgrowths of the large petals (see arrows in illustration).

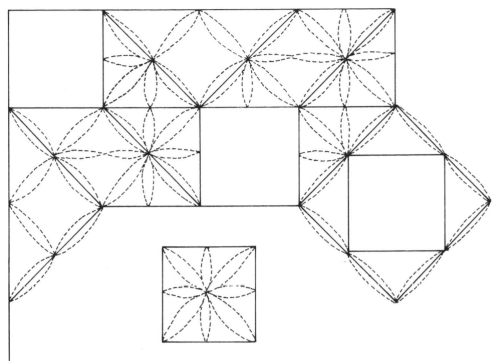

Quilting can be done continuously over the surface of the quilt, using several threaded needles at one time, each traveling in a diagonal direction.

The templates for the *Star Flower* quilting pattern appear on the following page.

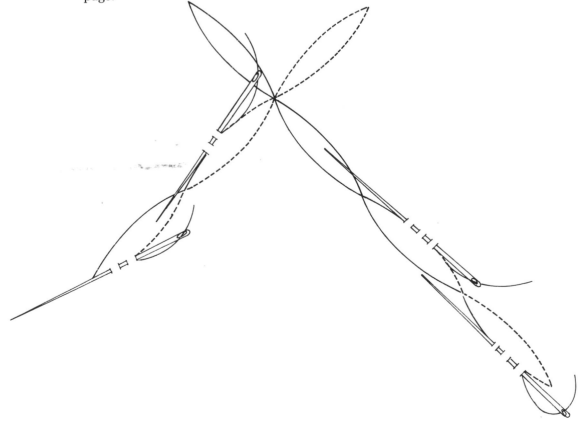

STAR FLOWER

2 templates

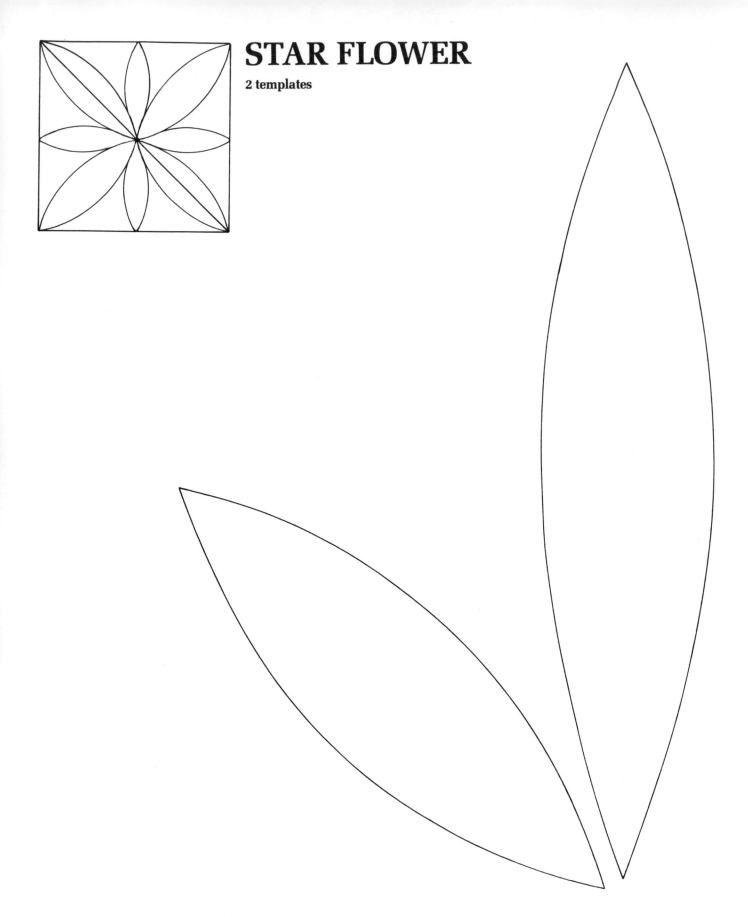

Binding

A binding covers and protects the raw edges of the quilt sandwich. There are many ways to bind a quilt, and the one used for the friendship quilt is called the bias method.

The Bias Method

Bias binding is the most sturdy and serviceable of all bindings and is sewn in 2 stages: first to the quilt top and then to the backing. Bias tape can be store-bought but handmade double-bias binding is stronger. It is easily attached by hand or machine to the finished quilt top, or later, when the sandwiching procedure is complete.

To make handmade bias cut fabric on the bias into 2″ wide strips. Join them diagonally to create a continuous band that is 4″-6″ longer than the perimeter of the quilt.

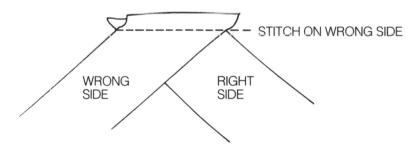

Fold the band lengthwise with wrong sides together. Sew (by hand using the running stitch or by machine using the straight stitch) onto the quilt top sides, leaving a 2"-3" tail at the beginning and end of the continuous band. Stop sewing 3"-4" from every corner and leave excess binding loops at the corners for later use.

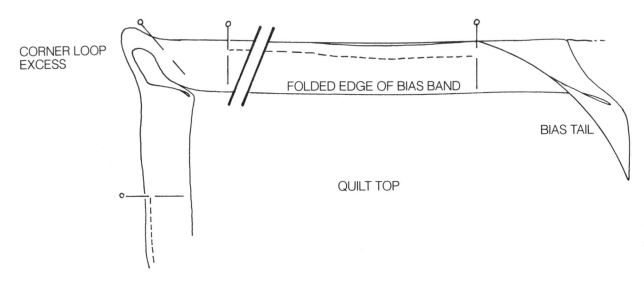

When the two bias ends meet, open the bands to their full width, place the beginning diagonal edge on top of the end band, and pin them together.

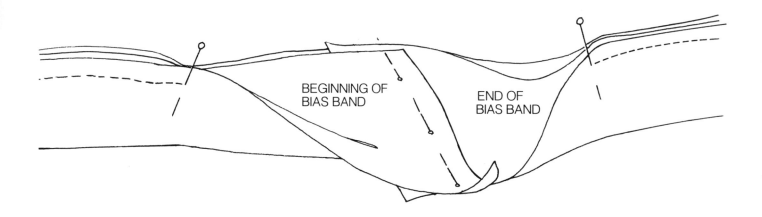

Using the diagonal raw edge as a guide, draw a pencil line on the wrong side of the end band.

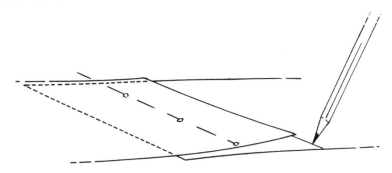

Remove pins and fold back top bias band. Mark a sewing line ¼″ away from the pencil line on bottom bias band, and a cut line ¼″ away from the sewing line.

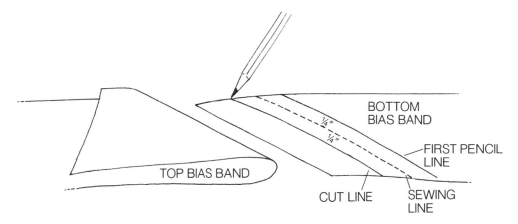

Join diagonal ends, right sides together, and stitch along the sewing line.

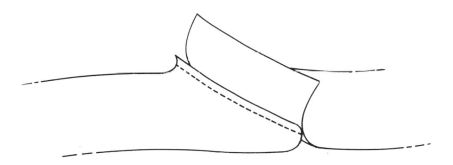

Check to see that the bias band lies flat on the quilt, then cut the excess off of the end band.

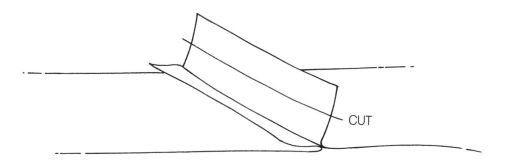

Thumb-press this seam open before folding the 2 raw edges onto the quilt top seam allowance for sewing. This completes the first stage of the bias binding application. Before the second stage begins on the backing of the quilt, the corners are squared.

SQUARELY BOUND CORNERS

The bias band has been sewn to within 3″-4″ of every corner, leaving room to maneuver the loops. Place pins at the ends of 2 sides at the corner with their respective bands. Make marks at the pinholes. Join the 2 marks with a single pin, then draw a right angle from this pin to the middle of the folded band and to the fold.

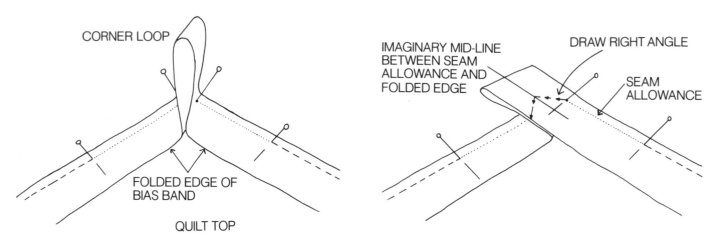

Hand-stitch on this right-angle line, then trim to within a ½″ beyond to test the corner by turning it inside out. If the corner fits snugly, it can be turned back again to trim to a ¼″ seam away from the drawn line. Only occasionally does the stitching need adjustment. After creating the squarely bound corner, stitch the bias up to the corner and around the corner to where stitching left off. After you have worked through this process on the first corner, the other corners can be squared immediately, thus promoting uniformity. Once stitched to the quilt top sides and corners, the bias is rolled to the back and the folded side blind-stitched in place.

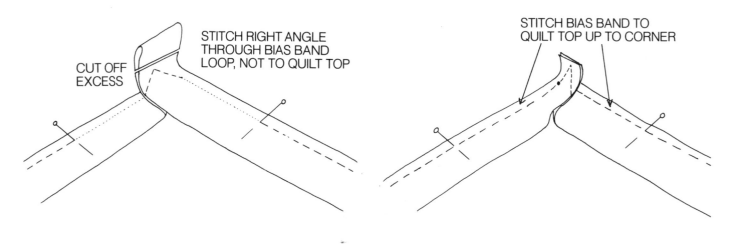

ADAPTATIONS OF SEWING BIAS BY GROUPS

When sewing bias, 4 people, 1 to a side, can sew the continuous length of bias on a quilt or quilt top at one time, thus drastically reducing the time involved. This group process applies only to the first and second stages of the bias binding; the 4 corners are best sewn by 1 person.

A table larger than the quilt project itself is the ideal surface upon which to bind a quilt, because the binding process takes too long to make the floor a suitable choice.

The Personal Touch

A friendship quilt is special for the very reasons surrounding its making. Equally special are the memories evoked by names, dates, or sayings written on the quilt. All of the designs in this book have space available to accommodate initials and dates; some even lend themselves to sayings. Most designs can be adapted by a slight change in color choice or by fusing templates to allow for more writing space. (See page 135 for examples of modified patterns.)

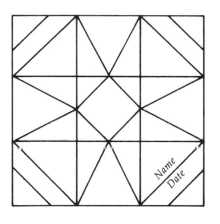

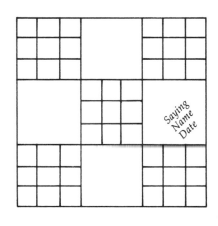

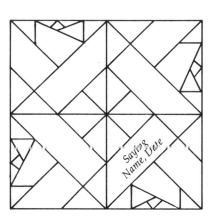

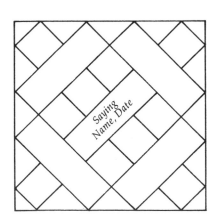

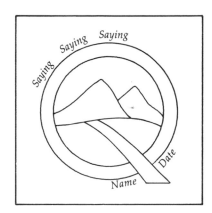

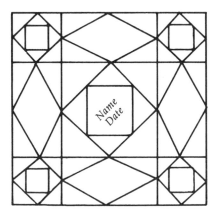

There are 3 elements to consider when signing a quilt block — where, what, and how to write. All 3 must blend harmoniously. After deciding where and what to write, take the template that will contain the writing and draw it on paper several times. Writing within the space, experiment with the placement and the size of the letters. Then center the writing. The space must not appear cramped by what is written and what is written must be legible.

PRACTICE SHEET

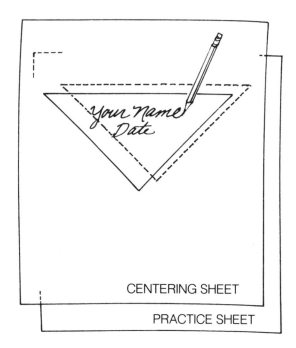

CENTERING SHEET

PRACTICE SHEET

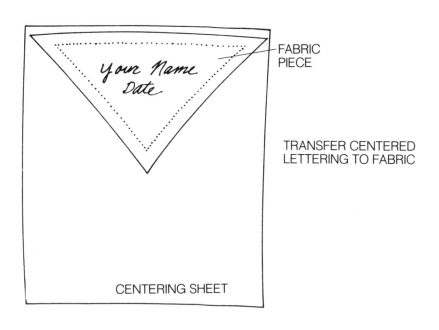

FABRIC PIECE

TRANSFER CENTERED
LETTERING TO FABRIC

CENTERING SHEET

If you already know how to embroider, consider using a fine stitch of outline, chain, backstitch, or cross stitch for the writing.

OUTLINE STITCH *Name*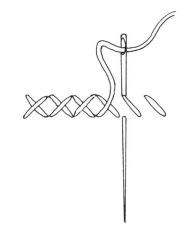

CHAIN STITCH *Name*

BACKSTITCH NAME

CROSS STITCH NAME

If you enjoy lettering and have a pen and indelible ink, the many forms of this art provide other options. In every case, making practice pieces is highly recommended. When using pen and indelible ink, first test the pen's point on the fabric. Some points pick up lint, which makes the ink spread. After writing on the sample piece of fabric, soak it in warm water for half an hour, then dry and press it. If the ink holds, you can be assured that it will remain permanently.

	SCRIPT	PRINT
CALLIGRAPHY PEN	*Name*	**NAME**
CROW QUILL PEN	*Name*	NAME
TECHNICAL PEN	*Name*	NAME

In all cases, lettering should be lightly drawn onto the fabric before you employ the permanent method of writing. The practice paper lettering can be darkened enough to show through some fabrics. For fabric that can't be seen through, place dressmaker's carbon under the practice paper and on top of the fabric, then trace over the writing.

MODIFIED PATTERNS

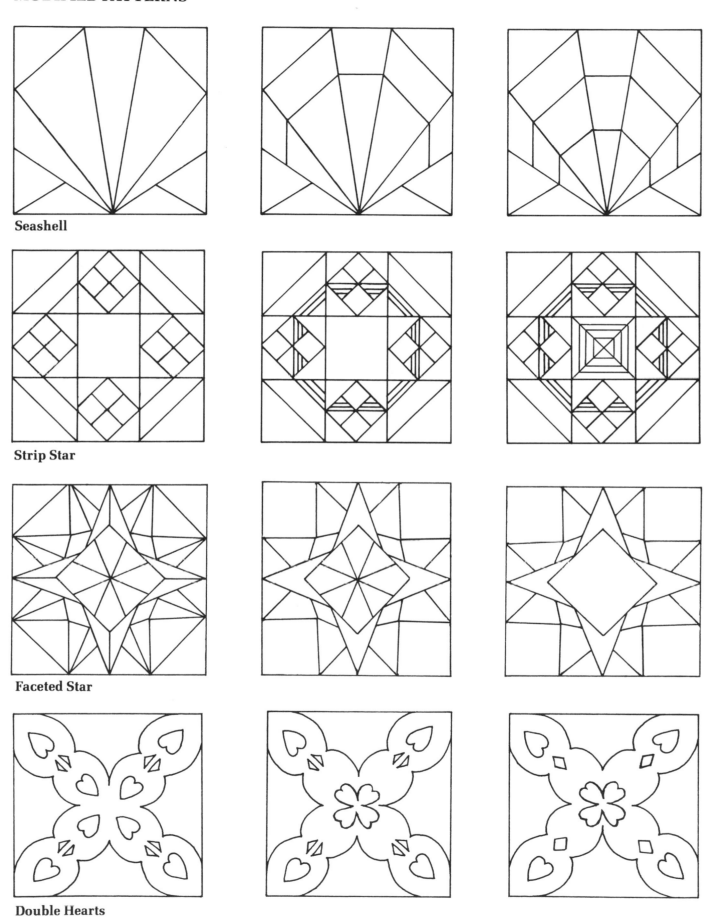

Seashell

Strip Star

Faceted Star

Double Hearts

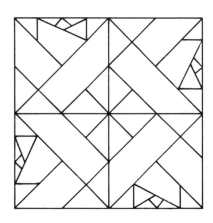

A friend is someone lovely who
Cut her chrysanthemums for you
And, giving, cares not for the cost,
Nor sees the blossoms she has lost;
But, rather, values friendship's store
Gives you her best and grows some more.
                                    Eleanor Long

Organizing a Friendship Quilt Project

Although the following discussion focuses on the quilt as a gift to a friend, the basic points would also apply to a quilt that was made as a fund-raiser to be raffled or auctioned off.

Nothing is more important to a group project than basic desire, but there is a big difference between desire and doing. To successfully complete a friendship quilt, you and the others involved must be willing to commit both time and energy to the project, as well as share your enthusiasm. When a group of any kind, however loosely structured, focuses on a common goal, organization is critical.

Some people may have doubts about their sewing ability or the time commitment and therefore cast a negative vote about joining. But these concerns are often dispelled once you have clearly defined the project's guidelines.

When groups of friends gather with a common desire to create a friendship quilt, the dynamics of the group process really begin. From the assembled group, key personalities emerge naturally. Certain people's inherent qualities make them well suited for certain specific jobs. The person most responsible for having verbalized the idea of creating a friendship quilt is often called the "instigator," but this person may not have the organizational skills required to complete her idea.

The roles of instigator, organizer, and hostess, although not directly related to sewing skill, are nevertheless vital to the success of a friendship quilt group project. Hostessing is important because the environment must provide comfortable working conditions. But if the instigator becomes the organizer, and slips into the hostess job as well, progress on the quilt may grind to a halt with the overload.

Organizational skills include the ability to listen to ideas and to develop from them a structure that best fits the group's needs. A good organizer feels comfortable in gathering people together, focusing their attention and channeling their enthusiasm for the project. The organizer is the person best suited to determine the size of the project, the number of friends needed, the financial requirements, the space available, and the time frame. If she is familiar with the people assembled, she can probably discern who the procrastinators, the followers, and the leaders are.

Organizational Elements

1. CHOOSING THE APPROPRIATE GIFT

Knowing your special friend's wants and needs will help in deciding upon the gift, which is best done by consensus. A bed-sized quilt in a new home or newly decorated room serves well, as does a wall quilt in your friend's favorite colors, or a lap quilt made of fabrics gleaned from a variety of friends' scrapbags.

2. PROJECT SIZE AS IT RELATES TO NUMBER OF FRIENDS

Does the number of friends coincide with the size of the project? Probably the more important element here is the number of friends. No one willing to work on a friendship quilt should ever be discouraged from participating. Opt for a larger project, if necessary, but be sure that the number of friends corresponds to the actual number of workers. The organizer who really knows her friends' strengths and weaknesses can best gauge their potential for work. She should be alert to tensions between friends and work around them.

3. THE SEWING SKILLS REQUIRED

Will the sewing and organizational skills of this group be adequate to accomplish the project? Has an honest appraisal been made of the project's degree of difficulty? Does some revision need to be made, or will experienced needlewomen be available to help novices? Will the experienced members of the group feel pressured by the extra demand for their time? If ¾ of the friends assembled know how to sew and a quarter of that group are quiltmakers, then the ones who are totally new to sewing will find the atmosphere conducive to learning, as long as those who are more experienced freely share their skills. If the size of the project or the complexity of the patterns sends waves of hesitation throughout the group, address the matter quickly. Alternatives may be to reduce the overall project size or to simplify the patterns (see page 135 for simplifying patterns).

Skill and time are important factors when deciding whether to finish the project by tieing or quilting. It is farfetched to imagine that a whole group of nonquilters would tackle and complete an entire quilting project by themselves. It can surely be done, but this might be an unfair expectation of your group; for although the quilting technique is basically simple, it's somewhat awkward at first. Two or 3 experienced quilters can add inspiration, but just remember that the quilting process will take appreciably longer than will the tieing of a quilt.

There is this thought, too. The finished quilt top in itself encompasses the thoughts, work, and fabric of friends, and as such is a perfectly acceptable gift. If the honored friend is a quilter herself, she may wish to quilt the top. Perhaps the time spent will rekindle memories of each participant. On the other hand, if your friend has no quilting skills and is unlikely to hold a quilting party, the quilt top in its unfinished state may be a burden.

4. TIME COMMITMENTS Considering your friends' other commitments, can they realistically give the time needed, working both as a group and individually, that this project requires? Some of the work and decisions must be shared at meetings; some can be accomplished by either 1 person or smaller (satellite) groups. Some of the solitary work is quite mobile and can be transported to meetings of other kinds, or done while traveling on public transportation, during long evenings at home, or while waiting for almost anything or anyone. Group time, however, is time away from family responsibilities.

For simplicity's sake, let us assume that the average person has a full-time job plus family responsibilities, and that the commitment to this project is based on sewing 1 block; sharing in the decisions for fabric choice, design, and format; piecing part of the quilt top together; and being a part of the finishing process (tieing or quilting). Whatever the size of the quilt, at least 3 group gatherings will be necessary, and most of these will probably be during evenings. These gatherings will last from 3 to 4 hours and will span a period of 2 to 4 months. Any shorter time does not allow for delays, and any longer time saps one's enthusiasm.

Beyond the group meetings, expect to work at home alone or in smaller groups for much of the sewing work. This time will entail anywhere from 1 to 5 hours sewing the chosen block, 4 to 6 hours piecing the top together, and 4 to 6 hours quilting and finishing the project.

5. GATHERINGS The proximity of your friends to one another will determine the number of group meetings. As a rule, the greater the distance, the fewer the group meetings and the greater the job of organization.

If members live within a 30-mile radius of each other, chances are that 3 main gatherings and some satellite meetings with carpooling will work best. Adequate space and a willing hostess will be needed for these — try to rotate the responsibilities.

When distances separate friends, concise correspondence provides an invaluable link. Then the organizer plus a close group of 3 to 4 friends can make the group decisions, purchase the supplies, assemble the quilt top, and alert others as to progress on and completion of the quilt. Main gatherings can be presented in a "party" atmosphere to attract distant friends, and might even include accommodations for an overnight. In any event, distances over 30 miles put the tasks of organization and assembly squarely on the shoulders of the organizer.

During the first meeting, the following should be accomplished:
1. Agree on an appropriate project.
2. Note any deadlines.
3. Estimate costs per person.
4. Choose a color scheme and discuss fabric choice.
5. Decide on a method of signing the quilt.
6. Choose a 'set' fabric and a 'set'.
7. Choose patterns.
8. Decide whether or not to use a quilting frame.
9. Select friends to:
    a. Purchase the 'set' fabric, backing, and batting.
    b. Launder the 'set' fabric and backing fabric.
    c. Cut the 'set' fabric and piece the backing (if need be).
10. Review the project; ask for questions; and arrange the time, date, and location of the next meeting.

The purpose of the second meeting is to regroup, note progress, note individual problems, and maintain a flexibility that allows for variables. Optimistically, all blocks should now have been sewn, 'set' fabrics prepared and cut, and other materials purchased, so that this is a working time, with piecing the quilt top the major concern. Depending on the time limitations of this gathering, the number of people present, and the size of the project, the quilt top may or may not be totally completed. Further work may be required of a smaller group, and names may need to be embroidered now, too.

The pressing of the completed quilt top and its preparatory basting with the batt and backing is best left to a smaller "satellite" meeting of 3 to 4 people. Between meetings 2 and 3, an invitation should be sent to your honored friend, for the third meeting will really be a party where the quilt (in an unfinished form — either the quilt top alone or sandwiched) will be presented. Quilting may begin at this party, but it surely won't be finished. Make preparations before the party for later quilting and binding of the quilt.

6. COSTS Finances are always a consideration, but they need not be prohibitive. Soon after you have established the size of the project and estimated the number of friends, you can calculate a rough cost per person.

Costs to anticipate include fabrics, batting, and thread for the quilt; correspondence by phone, postcard, and letter; and meeting expenses of food, drink, paper products, and space.

Using this friendship quilt as an example, the costs were as follows:

Materials purchased	$ 56.00
Scraps donated	-0-
Correspondence	$117.00
Meetings	$ 50.00
Total	$223.00

When all was totaled, then divided by the number of participants, each friend contributed approximately $7.00 and 20 hours of time within a 4-month time span.

Ways to Cut Costs

A. Note that the largest expenses by far were incurred for correspondence. You can reduce that amount substantially through careful organization. Although personal contact and phone calls are the most satisfying means of approach, a letter with a return postcard is the most effective way to contact distant friends with all of the particulars of the project. A sample follows:

Dear Margot,

As you probably have heard by now, our friend Vivian has left our area with her family to build a new home in Colorado. Their plans call for decorating their place with all kinds of craft work. So my thoughts have turned to making her a bed-sized quilt. It would be wonderful for all of us if we could share in her new home.

If this sounds like an idea that you could join in for the next few months, please return the enclosed postcard before the meeting date.

Sincerely,

Mary

The Postcard

☐ Yes, I wish to participate in the project.
☐ I will attend the January 21 meeting at your home at 1 PM.
☐ I will not be able to participate.

My skills and support are in the areas of:
☐ Hostessing   ☐ Space   ☐ Food   ☐ Sewing
☐ Piecing   ☐ Appliquéing   ☐ Embroidering
☐ Quilt Top Assembly   ☐ Quilting   ☐ Tieing
☐ Moral Support   ☐ Financial Support

Name _____ Phone _____
Address _____
_____

As the organizer gathers the returned postcards and notes the number of participants, their skills, and their areas of support, she can eventually determine an appropriate project size. Thus the first gathering will have a solid structure from which to begin group planning.

B. If half of the group are quiltmakers, their bountiful scrapbags will not only contribute fabrics that are precious to the participants, but at the same time help reduce the fabric yardage costs. (The major expenses connected with material costs remain the 'set' fabrics, the batting, and the backing fabric, all of which must be new, of good quality, and carefully prepared for the project. There should be no cost-cutting here.)

C. Space need not be a problem or an expense for a large gathering. Consider the local park, weather permitting, for a picnic gathering, or the local library's function room. At home, space may be at a premium and seats in even shorter supply; suggest that your friends bring beach chairs or pillows for comfort, for nothing spoils a meeting faster than numb posteriors.

As for food, plan on potluck for all occasions; or to reduce the importance of food altogether, there is always the bag lunch. However, if time permits the indulgence of food, a creative hand in the kitchen can be a great inducement to attend meetings.

Somewhere between coffee and wine, this popular quilter's drink is the perfect complement to any food plan.

Shan D. Lear's Iced Tea for Friends

3 quarts water
12 tea bags tied together
1/4 cup sugar
12-ounce can frozen orange juice concentrate, plus 3 cans water
6-ounce can frozen lemonade concentrate, plus 3 cans water
6-ounce can frozen limeade concentrate, plus 3 cans water
10 to 12 fresh mint leaves

Bring the water to a boil, add the tea bags and sugar, and stir until the sugar has dissolved. Let steep 15 minutes. Add the reconstituted fruit juices and the mint leaves, stir, and refrigerate until thoroughly chilled.

7. DEADLINES   The whole idea of a friendship quilt may revolve around a key date. The date may be one of departure, of birth, or of some other change. Dates such as these in anyone's life set the adrenalin flowing, and a special pace begins — one that can sometimes generate the energy needed to complete a friendship quilt in a shorter time than ever expected. In fact, some people work better with deadlines, for this helps eliminate procrastination.

When working on a group project of any size, anticipate delays no matter how critical the deadline, and expect some procrastination even from the best of friends; both are a part of any project. Working with the excitement of completion as a group can be exhilarating, yet the very best of groups can suffer from the strain of pressure when individuals begin to voice dissent about being overworked.

No part of creating a friendship quilt need ever be unpleasant, however. The aim of this book is to guide you through the quilt-making process. At the same time, you will be preserving happy memories and personal sentiments in a material form.

Glossary

ANCHOR   a "third-hand" device used in piecing patchwork to allow the sewing hand more freedom (see page 92)

ANCHOR STITCH   a stationary stitch used to reinforce a weak area of appliqué, such as an acute point or a cleft

APPLIQUÉ (noun)   the design created by sewing fabric shapes onto one another and/or onto a base fabric block

(verb)   the act of blind-stitching fabric shapes to a base fabric block

BACKSTITCH   a special running stitch used at the beginning and end of a line of stitching to reinforce it

BASE BLOCK   the fabric square upon which fabric shapes are placed and sewn to form the appliqué pattern

BASTING   the long temporary running stitches used to keep pieces of a pattern secure before permanent stitches are taken; also used to secure the sandwiched layers of a quilt before quilting begins

BATT or BATTING   the polyester middle layer between the quilt top and the backing fabric, which adds thickness as well as warmth to the finished quilt

BINDING   any one of a number of ways to finish off the raw edges of a quilt, uniting the sandwiched layers

BLIND STITCH   the basic stitch used for appliqué (see page 100)

BLOCK (noun)   the finished fabric design of patchwork or appliqué

(verb)   to make square by careful pressing

CALICO	a cotton or cotton-blend fabric with very small designs of one or many colors
ECOLOGY CLOTH	an unbleached, permanent-press, solid muslin fabric
FABRIC COLOR WHEEL	an aid in determining fabric colors on hand, their relationship within a given color, and their relationship with one another (see page 65)
FABRIC MAP	a sketch to determine the most efficient placement of templates on the fabrics to be used; also to determine the yardage required for a particular design, designs, or an entire quilt project
FLEXIBLE SEAM	a seam that has not been sewn in one direction or another, but simply by-passed by the running stitch
FIXED SEAM	a seam that has been turned in one direction and sewn in place by the running stitch
GUIDE CREASES	the folds — horizontal, vertical, and diagonal — in the base block fabric of an appliqué project used to center the fabric piece(s) of the appliqué design
PIECE (noun)	one fabric shape of an appliqué or patchwork design
(verb)	to sew, using the running stitch, 2 or more pieces together in a patchwork design
PREBASTING	a special step required of some appliqué shapes, used to keep raw edges turned under before appliquéing the shapes onto the base block
PREPARED FABRIC	fabric ready to be cut, having first been washed and ironed
PRESS SHEET	a fabric square with an exact drawing of the quilt block dimensions at its center, used to square up patchwork and appliqué blocks after they have been completed but before they are arranged into quilt form
QUILTING	the art of connecting the sandwiched layers of a quilt with a running stitch
QUILTING FRAME	a large apparatus consisting of poles or boards upon which an entire quilt is stretched for easy access in quilting
QUILTING HOOP	a "lap-sized" quilting frame, either round or oval in shape, which stretches and isolates only a small area to be quilted at one time
QUILT TOP	the top layer of a quilt, consisting of fabric appliqué and/or patchwork blocks (and sometimes 'set' fabrics) which are arranged together in finished size

REVERSE APPLIQUÉ (noun) denotes the special fabrics slipped between the base block and the appliqué pieces

(verb) the act of blind-stitching a fabric scrap shape underneath the opening(s) in a larger appliqué shape

SANDWICHING layering the backing, batting, and quilt top together in preparation for basting

SEAM ALLOWANCE that space between the drawn (sewing) line and the edge of a piece of fabric; the width may vary, but is usually around ¼″ for quiltmakers

'SET' the arrangement of the blocks used for a project; also, the fabric shapes used to physically separate yet visually unify the blocks included in a quilt or smaller project

STRIP-PIECING the sewing machine technique used to create "new" fabric by carefully sewing together narrow strips of fabric

TEMPLATE the shape of an appliqué or patchwork design cut out of a sturdy material such as clear plastic, metal, or mat board, and drawn around to create the fabric pieces

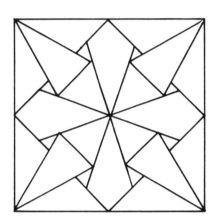

"While my work has ever been before me, my reward has always been with me."
Elder Frederick Evans
from *By Shaker Hands*
by June Sprigg

Bibliography

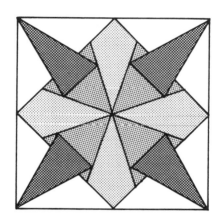

Beyer, Jinny. *Patchwork Patterns*. McLean, VA: EPM Publications, Inc., 1979.

Birren, Faber. *Color and Human Response*. New York: Van Nostrand Reinhold, 1978.
Color in Your World. New York: Macmillan, 1962.
Color Perception in Art. New York: Van Nostrand Reinhold, 1976.
Light, Color and Environment. New York: Van Nostrand Reinhold, 1982.

Block, Joel. *Friendship: How to Give it, How to Get It*. New York: Macmillan, 1980.

Eiseman, Leatrice. *Alive with Color*. Washington, D.C.: Acropolis Books, Ltd., 1983.

Fabian, Melanie & Sigal, Sandra. *Appliqué Album Quilts*. Irvine, CA: Gick Publishing, Inc., 1983.

Finley, Ruth. *Old Patchwork Quilts*. Newton Centre, MA: Charles T. Branford Co., 1929.

Gross, Joyce. *Quilters' Journal*. Mill Valley, CA.

Grossman, Richard. "Prescription for a Long and Healthy Life." *Family Health*, February, 1981.

Hall, Carrie & Kretsinger, Rose. *The Romance of the Patchwork Quilt*. New York: Bonanza Books, 1935.

Hassel, Carla J. *You Can Be a Super Quilter*. Des Moines, IA: Wallace-Homestead Book Co., 1980.

Houck, Carter & Miller, Myron. *American Quilts and How to Make Them*. New York: Charles Scribner's Sons, 1975.

Irwin, John R. *A People and Their Quilts*. Exton, PA: Schiffer Publishing, Ltd., 1983.

James, Michael. *The Quiltmaker's Handbook*. Englewood Cliffs, NJ: Prentice-Hall, Inc., 1978.
The Second Quiltmaker's Handbook. Englewood Cliffs, NJ: Prentice-Hall, Inc., 1981.

Laury, Jean Ray. *The Creative Woman's Getting-It-All-Together at Home Handbook*. New York: Van Nostrand Reinhold, 1977.

Lawson, Suzy. *Amish Inspirations*. Cottage Grove, OR: Amity Publications, 1982.

Lehman Publications. *Quilter's Newsletter Magazine*. Wheatridge, CO.

McLoughlin, John C. "The Sisterhood of the Hive." *Country Journal*, July, 1982, pp. 58-65.

Orlofsky, Myron & Patsy. *Quilts in America*. New York: McGraw-Hill Book Co., 1974.

Robbins, Judy. *Hands All Around: Making Cooperative Quilts*. New York: Van Nostrand Reinhold, 1984.

Sherberg, Ellen. "Beautiful Are Friends." *Parents Magazine*, March, 1982, pp. 47-50.

Sprigg, June. *By Shaker Hands*. New York: Alfred A. Knopf, 1975.

Swift, Henry & Elizabeth. *Community Groups and You*. New York: The John Day Co., 1964.

NOTES

True friendship foresees the needs of others rather than proclaims its own.

André Maurois

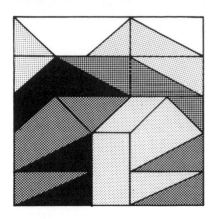

NOTES

Friendship, compounded of esteem and love, derives from one its tenderness and its permanence from the other.
Samuel Johnson

NOTES

*A true friend is somebody who
can make us do what we can.*
Ralph Waldo Emerson

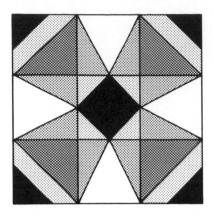

NOTES

*A friend is a neighbor
of the heart.*

Blanche Harris